INTERNATIONALISATION OF POST-1992 UK UNIVERSITIES

Internationalisation
OF POST-1992 UK
UNIVERSITIES

THE GOOD, THE BAD AND
THE UGLY

PETER BRADY

ANTHEM PRESS

Anthem Press
An imprint of Wimbledon Publishing Company
www.anthempress.com

This edition first published in UK and USA 2020
by ANTHEM PRESS
75–76 Blackfriars Road, London SE1 8HA, UK
or PO Box 9779, London SW19 7ZG, UK
and
244 Madison Ave #116, New York, NY 10016, USA

British Library Cataloguing-in-Publication Data
A catalogue record for this book is available from the British Library.

Library of Congress Cataloging-in-Publication Data
Library of Congress Control Number: 2019955630

ISBN-13: 978-1-78527-116-8 (Hbk)
ISBN-10: 1-78527-116-4 (Hbk)

This title is also available as an e-book.

CONTENTS

PREFACE

With Brexit still uncertain as I write, the place of the UK in the modern international world is unclear. What is sure is that it will change fundamentally over the coming years. How our universities and graduates are ready for this change is of national and personal interest. This book looks at the UK government's internationalisation strategies from the point of view of post-1992 universities. It investigates why post-1992 universities in the UK internationalised, how they went about it and what were the effects on the universities, their local environment and the major countries they operated in.

This book compares the UK government's internationalisation strategies with that of the UK university sectors' major markets, China, Malaysia and the United States, and investigates how post-1992 universities have helped these countries internationalise, receiving little in return but short-term monetary gain.

I have not counted the EU as a major international market in this text. This is partly because of the uncertainty around Brexit, which will potentially allow a book by itself to be written about UK universities' relationships with the EU and partly because post-1992 universities have always treated the EU as a home market.

Over the period that this book spans, the understanding of the internationalisation of higher education has matured and changed. In 2015, Jane Knight, updating the definition of internationalisation, stated that 'it is important that a definition does not specify the rationales, benefits, outcomes, actors, activities, or stakeholders of internationalization as these elements vary across nations and from institution to institution' (Knight 2015).

This book attempts to do just that across a section of the UK higher education sector –namely post-1992 universities. For the purposes of this book, the term internationalisation is used to describe any activity that is carried out by universities that have an international component.

Internationalisation of Post-1992 Universities is not a purely academic tome but what my publishers classify as a 'crossover'.

But in developing my arguments I have tried to do so with a proper evidence base and not relied on anecdotal stories. I have also tried to give a true account of how UK universities have operated in different markets over time.

Although it is now common to discuss UK higher education as a single sector, I argue that this is not the case. The history of post-1992 universities, as depicted in Chapters 1 to 3, show that these universities were and are fundamentally different from pre-1992 universities, they had poorer funding, weaker governance and less commercial potential. This has translated into a group of universities more likely to take risks when developing business overseas. That is not to say that all post-1992 universities have taken risks or that no pre-1992 university has.

In the book the mistakes of certain post-1992 universities are mentioned more than others. This should not be taken as evidence that they are particularly aggressive risk-takers. It may be that they were the ones that were naive and were caught out. Likewise, those which are shown to have developed innovative programmes for the good of all students may not be complete paragons of virtue.

I hope you enjoy reading this book and that many of you recognise the story and environment that I describe and have worked in for the majority of my working life.

PROLOGUE

International education it's nothing new. For centuries British universities have taught the progeny of despots, sons of rajas, terrorists–who when they won their fight became the fathers of a new nation; they all came to the dreaming spires to study, mingle and be Anglicised.

They returned home replete with swan stuffed with widgeon and happy memories of a Britain still at the top of its game, where the plebs knew their place, punters were people with punts and all was right with the world.

It was all about using university education of foreign nationals to exert soft power. So when they become leaders in their countries, Britain was their first-choice partner to split the proceeds of their invasion of some oil rich neighbour. Or the supplier of choice of those wonderfully clever anti-personnel mines and other weapons of indiscriminate and discriminate mass murder that we make so well.

Of course, when Thatcher changed the rules and universities could charge full fees for international students, there developed a more commercial approach to international recruitment. But it was very much a peripheral activity for universities. With the creation of a whole new group of universities in 1992, the cosy world of international education in the UK changed dramatically.

For the new post-1992 universities, hawking their wares overseas was the only way their vice chancellors could get enough non-exchequer income to make up for years of underinvestment and to fund the expansion in student numbers the government demanded. Post-1992 universities developed differently than their predecessors. With pressure from the previous polytechnic directors the new universities had been set up as a commercial body with expensive CEOs who had a managerial style to suit a dynamic entrepreneurial business rather than an accountable public body.

The directors had made sure that the new boards of governors were toothless and they could do anything they wanted with their shiny new institutions – so there was little or no oversight of their overseas activities. Salary increases of eye-watering proportions were ratified by remuneration committees that the vice chancellors sat on.

Simultaneously, from the 1990s on, successive governments encouraged the sale of university qualifications overseas, using them as advance economic troops in attempts to attract businesses to the UK. They were one of the first businesses invited by the government to join trade missions in newly opened markets.

Almost every university in the UK ramped up international recruitment activities. But for new universities with little pedigree, to be successful in a world where education was increasingly monetised, so called innovative strategies were needed.

Staff from universities from the Scotland Highlands to the South Coast of England descended on Kuala Lumpur, Tripoli and other capital cities throughout the world, like latter-day missionaries, bringing the natives salvation in the form of Western education.

Universities took their lead on which countries and regimes to do business with from the government of the time, rather than making their own moral judgements. If it's okay for the British government to do business, there can't be any moral issues – can there?

So they ignored any negative reports of their new-found partners.

Institutions that denounced any form of discrimination based on racial, religious or sexual orientation found themselves taking money from governments, with quite different morals and ethics. Senior staff in universities watched TV reports about genocide, imprisoning of academics, mass re-education policies or just plain murder in countries where they had just signed partnership agreements as fulsome as a B-list celebrities' wedding vows.

From the 1990s and into the new century, excess followed excess and the money piled in. Executive lounges in five star hotels were full of surprisingly badly dressed guests, as the international education horde realised that the free drink that one got as part of the luxury executive package did not appear on the hotel bill. So the university would pay and never question it.

Senior academics who would never be able to pay for this luxury took full advantage; meetings had to end by 5 pm to accommodate the free cocktail hour. To be fair, the more conscientious held meetings in the executive lounges during the cocktail hour.

Professors of sustainable energy dusted off their Hawaiian shirts and hit Hard Rock Cafes from Sao Paulo to Saigon, where their true attractiveness was apparent to young ladies and lady boys who were not as shallow as their Western counterparts.

Old academics fell asleep with their heads in recently emptied minibars. Staff tipexed the 'a' out of 'massage' on hotel bills and replaced it with an 'e' – back home, accounts staff were shocked at how much a message could cost in some countries never mind the 'extras'.

Heads of business schools who had never had to demonstrate a head for business took to the new concept of universities as cash generators with a vengeance. This was the chance to show that the old adage 'those that can do, those that can't teach' was wrong.

They became institutionalised entrepreneurs – not unlike the bankers and traders who were doing so well for the world economy at the time. They were able to risk other people's money with no risk to themselves. And in what was considered by marketing men as a soft market, there was every chance that the risk would bring in significant monetary rewards.

Engineers who had spent time in industry before they became academics in the local polytechnics found themselves becoming what they had always despised most – salesmen. They amassed millions of air miles, stayed in particular chains of hotels which had loyalty points and never had to pay for a holiday for their families again.

Doormen in Mandarin Orientals, Shangri Las, Sandals Resorts and Tajs knew them by name, but never got a tip as that wasn't refundable by the university.

And all the time these business heads were lauded as heroes by the press as, overnight, education became one of Britain's largest export sectors.

A whole new career path opened up for clever young people who had studied languages at university and then realised that having English as your native language and an intimate knowledge of the modern literature of another language was of no interest to industry. After all, whatever language you studied had millions of native speakers of which a rising number spoke English fluently and many had an actual useful skill – like engineering or computing, rather than just being able to translate someone else's words.

So, finding no work outside teaching other languages to students who, like themselves, would find no work, they flocked to join the new profession of international recruitment officer. It was these young people who flew like sardines, common class, stayed in cheap hotels and went to danger spots that you would never get a senior member of staff to visit – Pakistan, Afghanistan, Nigeria, Yemen and so on – these were the people that actually recruited hundreds of thousands of overseas students into UK universities.

Agencies opened all over the world to dip their beaks in the fountain of money produced. These middlemen represented large numbers of universities. The funding from international students was so important to new universities that for the majority of staff, who stayed at home manning the fort, it felt as if chasing international income was prioritised over teaching. A new form of institution had developed, one where students were markets and programmes were products.

True to their roots, new universities proved to be incredibly flexible in entry requirements; after all, if they could take UK students into degrees with low grades and alternative qualifications and still pass them, why would they demand more of foreign students?

This meant that they took in more students into advanced years then pre-1992 universities. In some cases British students returning to final year of their degree found that instead of classes of 20 UK students they had a hundred new foreign colleagues none of whom could buy a packet of crisps without using sign language but who were taking modules on banking ethics – an oxymoron comparable to military intelligence.

Business schools grew to accommodate international students rather than because of any local or national need. Questions as to whether universities had a responsibility to their local population and whether UK students would be able to get jobs when competing with overseas students who had two languages and dual qualifications were derided as parochial – out of touch with the modern global world.

International education as a means of bringing income into underfunded universities and into many small cities throughout the UK was without doubt effective. The nature of not only the university but also its surrounding communities was changed for the better with most of the country realising the economic and cultural benefits of this influx of temporary visitors. Media stories of how these temporary immigrants were contributing to cultural and economic growth were a beacon against the anti-immigration rants in some press. Small cities reeling from traditional industry closures found that the new local university was now the biggest employer in town and paid better with better conditions than before. The growth of these universities was only possible with income from international students.

In an era before Trump and Brexit, where internationalisation and globalisation were seen as not only inevitable but also desirable, this trade was a shining example of how everyone could benefit from the effects of an increasingly international world, but only if there was a way of using the new makeup of the university body to the benefit of home students.

Universities with their roots in public service realised that it could not be all about money. The concept of internationalisation at home was developed with mixed results. Internationalisation strategies were developed that tried to recognise and resolve the conflict between funding and education. They re-labeled 'international recruitment' to 'internationalisation' claiming it was less about the pounds and more about the people.

As the 1990s progressed through the noughties and into the teens, the swashbuckling behaviour that was created in the initial Klondike-like rush lessened, as staff and processes matured to take into account the hard lessons the sector learned.

When the government decided that on-campus international students should be at a level described in the International English Language Test as a 'Modest User who should be able to handle basic communication in their own field', the recruitment market slowed down, particularly for post-1992 universities.

To counter this downturn, many new universities began to focus on transnational education (TNE). Instead of Mohammed coming to the mountain the mountain would come to Mohammed.

UK university degree programmes were increasingly outsourced to private colleges and universities throughout the world.

The government agencies which were designed to ensure quality in the UK joined in, selling their own programmes or becoming onlookers and recorders rather than regulators.

And all the while the media failed to hold the sector to account. They were too busy publishing league tables, selling glossy adverts, writing university guides, even running recruitment events, to upset the apple cart.

In the last two and a half decades, post-1992 university activities overseas has influenced the commercial behaviour of all UK universities as pre-1992 universities allowed post-1992 universities to take the risks and then emulated those that they had got away with.

The focus of post-1992 universities on international student fees above all developed a market-led culture which many would say is at odds with a public body – this was easily translated to the fee regime in England when it was introduced.

This book looks at the undoubted success of post-1992 universities' international strategies and how this has changed them. It examines some of the practices they had to adopt and the consequences of doing so. It also looks at the effect of this on the countries they operate in and how they have been used by other cultures and nations to realise their own interpretation of internationalisation.

CHAPTER 1

THE POLYTECHNIC IDEAL – LOCAL, EQUAL TO UNIVERSITIES BUT DIFFERENT

THE NEED FOR NEW TYPES OF GRADUATES 1960S

The swinging 60s, the war was long finished, rationing was but a bad memory and there was a renewed optimism and increasing wealth. No longer the black and white of the 1950s, the 1960s were lived in technicolor.

Ordinary men and women were embracing the joys of instant mashed potatoes, coming to terms with eating spaghetti that didn't come out of a tin – do you use a spoon with your fork or not? They were moving to high-rise tower blocks with bathrooms and indoor toilets –some even had showers over the bath – buying their first car, first TV and first washing machines. Old-fashioned was bad and everything new was good. Polystyrene ceiling tiles, bright orange bri-nylon sheets, psychedelic shirts, drip-dry suits, the pill, the space race, the first heart transplant, the invention of Astro Turf all were greeted with enthusiasm. It was an exciting modern world, one where science and the new were embraced by everyday people. Affordable package holidays to exotic locations, which had previously needed a war for working-class Brits to visit, stretched global horizons. Britain applied to join the forerunner to the European Union (EU) – the European Economic Community (EEC) – twice in the 1960s, but was blocked by the French president Charles De Gaulle, who claimed that Britain harboured a 'deep-seated hostility towards European construction' (BBC On This Day, 1967). Post-Brexit he must be as smug in his grave as he was in life. But in the 1960s and 1970s there was a wide-held belief in the benefits of joining the EEC and being part of a new order, The 1960s were when Britain and its people had to assume a new place in a world without the British Empire.

Politicians recognised this was a new era. The heavy manufacturing that Britain had relied on was becoming less viable, the unions claiming that post-war owners had refused to reinvest, the owners claimed the unions were strangling investment with pre-war work practices.

At the start of the 1960s, the prime minister was Harold Wilson, a shifty political wheeler dealer; he was never entirely trusted, even by his own party. Tony Benn famously said, 'The tragedy of Harold Wilson was that you could never believe a word he said' (*The Telegraph* 2014). In later years, Anthony Howard in a leader in the *New Statesman* was to say that 'Mr Wilson has now sunk to a position where his very presence in Labour's Leadership pollutes the atmosphere of politics' (Kellner 2010).

But in 1963, Wilson made his 'White Heat of Technology' speech at the Labour Party conference. Undoubtedly, it was one of the most famous political speeches of the twentieth century. He concluded that, for Britain to prosper, 'a new Britain' would need to be forged in the 'white heat' of the 'scientific revolution' (Francis 2013). By focusing on science and not ideology, he managed to unite the previously divided party under the banner of a new scientific socialist party. In the same speech, he portrayed Conservatives as old Etonians, out of touch with the modern technological world (Francis 2013).

By the 1960s, it was widely recognised by all parties that the existing university system could not create the volume or indeed the type of graduates that such a scientific revolution required. However, not all felt that it was the place of universities to do so.

In 1959 the novelist and physical chemist C. P. Snow gave a Rede lecture entitled 'The Two Cultures and the Scientific Revolution'. He claimed that British social and political elites were dominated by 'natural Luddites', whose ignorance of science and engineering made them singularly unfit to govern a world in which technology was becoming ever more important. He argued, almost with disbelief, that not only were they Luddites, but they also reveled in their lack of knowledge of science and engineering as a sign of intelligence and breeding. And, of course, these elites were products of the old universities (Age of the Sage n.d.).

Like a character out of Tom Sharpe's satire on Oxbridge life 'Porterhouse Blue', F. R. Leavis, director of English at Downing College, Cambridge, and a well-known literary critic, made a waspish retaliation to Snow's criticism in his Richmond lecture, in which he called Snow 'intellectually as undistinguished as it was possible to be' and continued in much the same vein, saying that 'Snow displays an utter lack of intellectual distinction and an embarrassing vulgarity of style' (Age of the Sage n.d.).

This backfired and the press rounded on Leavis and his views, giving fuel to the debate about the role of traditional universities in a modern world.

What was widely accepted, outside Oxbridge, was that the country needed more people studying a wider range of subjects aligned with industry, seen as equivalent to a university degree. People were looking towards post-war France and Germany, where technocrats were running the country. From across the channel they appeared to be doing a far better job of modernising, creating joined-up road and rail networks and radical town planning. Of course, when the UK took some of their ideas, they found that high-rises built cheaply in bomb sites were not quite as glamorous as they had looked like in the sun of the Mediterranean and ultra-modern Bonn.

There were two opposing views of how the UK could develop a higher education sector that would produce a cadre of technocrats (Pratt 1997). On one side was Lord Lionel Robbins, a grammar-school boy who graduated from the London School of Economics. On the other side Mr, later, Sir Tobias Weaver, an old Cliftonian who had graduated from Cambridge. Robbins at the time was chair of the London School of Economics, he was an economist and an advocate of free-market economics. Weaver was a civil servant who, when he entered the civil service, had asked for a gentleman's agreement that he would never be moved from the department of education. Both were passionate about the need for participation in higher education to increase for Britain to be able to take advantage of the new post-war world. But whereas Robbins believed in increasing the numbers of universities to meet this market and allowing those universities to work in a free market, Weaver believed in a locally managed higher education system to deal with local industries and local people's needs.

THE ROBBINS REPORT

The Robbins Committee on Higher Education Report in 1963 (Robbins 1963) was instructed by the Conservative government to look at the higher education system in the UK and recommend its long-term development plans and in particular to look at

> whether any new types of institution are desirable and whether any modifications should be made in the present arrangements for planning and co-ordinating the development of the various types of institution. (Robbins 1963)

This was the first time there had ever been an attempt by government to review higher education in the UK as a whole rather than individual independent units. In fact, Robbins believed that it would be wrong to say there was a system of higher education at the time. He says in the report, 'Even today it would be a misnomer to speak of a system of higher education in this country, if by system is meant a consciously co-ordinated organisation' (Robbins 1963).

The development of higher education had for most part been carried out by the universities who had independent wealth. However, as Robbins pointed out, the financial situation of universities had changed and 'all depend on large grants from the state to enable them to carry out their present functions' (Robbins 1963) and much work that would be considered higher education was, by the 1960s, carried out with universities by the newly formed colleges of advanced technology's (CAT).

This was an opportunity to create a new type of system that was fit for the modern world – one which widened access in both socio-economic terms and gender. In particular, it was a chance to elevate what was considered vocational higher education to the same level as the study of humanities. It was a pivotal moment in the development of higher education in the UK, and the free-market economist Robbins did not rise to the challenge and advocated more of the same.

Robbins argued that a higher education system should be developed with co-ordination principles and common objectives while allowing institutional autonomy. He suggested that there should be 'free development of institutions', and 'existing institutions must be free to experiment without predetermined limitations' and any new institutions must have the same rights as existing ones (Robbins 1963, 139).

So basically, Robbins, the head of a university, was asked to write a report on how universities should be managed, and his view was that you should let the universities do whatever they want with no control – not really much of a surprise.

Although he was claiming to treat higher education as a system, it was one where the only control was some sort of unspecified market. He even recommended that the freedom at that time enjoyed by the universities from investigation of their books by the Comptroller and Auditor General should be extended to the other components of the new extended system. And tellingly, there was no section on existing and future interaction between higher education and industry. The report did not address the issue of how the free market would develop parity in status between vocational higher education and non-vocational education.

The report said that starting immediately, two new universities would be formed, with one in Scotland, the 10 colleges of advanced technology in

England and Wales would be given university status and the two similar colleges in Scotland.

Three years later, by 1966, under the Labour government at that time, all CATs had received their charter and became known as the plate-glass universities.

However, for Robbins this was just a start. He wanted any institution which provided higher education to be given the chance to form a university or join existing universities as separate departments. His view was of a single university sector comprising differing types and sizes of autonomous institutions. He expected that the next wave of universities would come from the regional colleges and central institutes (in Scotland) and suggested the creation of a central body, the Council for National Academic Awards (CNAA), to award degrees with a specific view to create an environment to help them develop the skills and experience, which would allow them to develop into universities.

The shape and nature of these new universities would not be driven by the centre or locally. He advocated institutional self-determination, which in his view would create a diverse higher education system. In effect Robbins was advocating a system largely funded by the state, which would have little or no control over the shape and nature of the sector.

THE WOOLWICH SPEECH

Robbins view of the free-market autonomous higher education system was killed in what is now known as the Woolwich speech (Crosland 1965). In this speech in 1965, Antony Crosland, the secretary of state for education and science announced the creation of polytechnics and what was to become known as the binary divide between universities and polytechnics. It has been claimed that he later said he regretted being bounced into making the Woolwich speech and that he was led by his officials and advisers to make it (Pratt 1997; Ratcliffe 2017). Perhaps they envisaged that the offices of the secretary of state for education and science operated like an episode of *Yes Minister* with Toby Weaver as Sir Humphrey and Antony Crosland as Jim Hacker.

> 'Well Toby, I think that's us finished for the day. I must say I'm rather pleased with that fellow Robbins report.' Crosland/Hacker may have said, at the end of a meeting,
>
> 'Yes Minister, There's just one thing Minister,' Sir Toby/Humphrey may have replied as he stood to leave.

'Yes Toby.'

'I'm afraid we can't go ahead with your planned speech tonight.'

'Why not?'

'It appears that the printers have broken.'

'Well get them fixed.'

'Ah, that's a problem, we can't find anyone who knows how.'

'What? There's no one can fix the bloody printers?'

'It appears not. They're very specialist pieces of equipment, state of the art, all the ministerial ones are linked in some way. Can't say I understand it myself.'

'For God's sake we employ the brightest and best, surely one of your young colleagues could do something.'

'fraid not all Classics and Greats knno to use with their hands I'm afraid minister'

'Still there's plenty of technicians in the bloody Palace of Whitehall. Surely someone can sort it out. We spend enough training the buggers.'

'That's the problem. We used to send them to the Woolwich College they did a special diploma. But they've stopped running the programme. Say they want to be a university so they are concentrating on Degree programmes only.'

'What. They're meant to provide trained staff for local needs.'

'Yes Minister. It's happening in colleges throughout the land. We're calling it academic drift.'

'Academic drift?'

'Yes Minister.'

'That doesn't sound good, does it Toby'?

'No Minister.'

'Can't have people thinking that we allow things to drift. That there's no one at the helm, can we?'

'No Minister.'

'What are we going to do about it?'

'Well Minister I have this speech here that you might want to use tonight.'

'Where?'

'Woolwich College Minister.'

Amusing as that scenario may be, the idea that Crosland would be pressured by his civil servants into creating a two-tier system of higher education is highly unlikely. If, in later years, Crosland claimed that he was bounced into making the speech, it is likely that as a consummate politician, he was trying to distance himself from the fact that through bad governance and underfunding, the polytechnic side of the binary divide had not delivered what he had hoped.

Crosland's Woolwich speech put the nail in the coffin of Robbins's view of multiple colleges and institutions becoming universities of equal status, developing, in a free market, without any state control, into whatever types of institutions they wished to be. Crosland laid out a vision of a two-tier system 'based on the twin traditions that have created our present higher education institutes' (Crosland 1965).

In his speech he suggested that a two-tier system would stop academic drift. To make it clear to the polytechnics that they were to stay on track, he stated that there would be no more universities created for at least 10 years – which actually turned out to be nearer 30 years.

The new polytechnics would produce vocational-, professional- and industry-based full-time and part-time courses at degree, just below degree and advanced levels. The teachers would have close links with industry, with many being industry professionals themselves, and the students would be committed to a profession at the outset. There should be more sandwich programmes, and while the main subjects would be scientific and technical, other professions such as social work and business management would be catered for. As new service industries that relied on these skills developed, he envisaged a complimentary system between the universities and polytechnics with some small areas of crossover.

Crosland decided that the polytechnics should be under local government control as it was 'desirable in itself that a substantial part of higher education should be under social control and directly responsible for social needs' (Crosland 1965).

WHAT CROSLAND WANTED THE POLYTECHNICS TO LOOK LIKE

Crosland's vision of the polytechnic sector as laid out in the Woolwich speech was one which developed graduates who could step straight into local industry and make a real immediate difference and one that carried out continued professional development – although that phrase had not been coined yet.

Polytechnics were to have parity with universities in terms of status and rigour and were to be under social control. He said, 'We shall not survive in this world if we in Britain alone down-grade the non-university professional and technical sector. No other country in the Western world does so [...] Let us now move away from our snobbish caste-ridden hierarchical obsession with university status' (Crosland 1965).

In this he was looking to the Grandes Ecoles in France and other centres of technical excellence throughout Europe, which were becoming increasingly more productive than the UK.

In the 1960s, the French system was binary in the same way as Crosland envisaged the UK one. In France there were universities and Grand Ecoles, with Grandes Ecoles teaching vocational subjects, mainly engineering and later businesses studies.

The majority of the presidents of France and its cabinet have been graduates of the Grande Ecoles, with the top Grande Ecole being the Ecole Polytechnic. In France, to this day, the majority of the people running large corporations and the country are technocrats. The term 'Ingénieur Diplomé' (graduate engineer) is a reserved title and until the 1970s could only be issued from a Grandes Ecole. Anyone misusing this title in France can be fined and even jailed.

It was to this model that Crosland looked to when he created the binary divide –one which would solve the issue that C. P. Snow had highlighted in his Rede lecture where he condemned the British higher education system for over-rewarding the humanities and under-rewarding the sciences, which 'in practice deprived British elites (in politics, administration, and industry) of adequate preparation to manage the modern scientific world' (Pratt 1997). It was not as it is now portrayed, intended to be a way in which the class system was perpetuated. Polytechnics were intended to have equal status and attract students who would have the choice of whether to attend university or polytechnic. Even the name polytechnic was originally meant to symbolise an elite as in the French system. To imagine that Crosland would deliberately develop a class system in higher education as the argument eventually became belies the nature of the man. He had already dismantled the binary system of school education, which he considered to be class-driven, where the top 20 per cent went to grammar schools and the remaining 80 per cent to secondary moderns. In her biography, Crosland's wife quoted him as saying, 'If it's the last thing I do, I'm going to destroy every fucking grammar school in England. And Wales and Northern Ireland' (Crosland 1982, 123), and he went on to do so. The story of why polytechnics did not realise their potential is also the story of how as universities post-1992, they still remain a distinct sector within UK higher education, despite strenuous claims to the contrary.

WHAT POLYTECHNICS ENDED UP AS

The 1970s

The 1970s was the decade where the reality of a post-war Britain without the influence and affluence of empire began to bite. Foreign competitors not only caught up but also overtook in quality, productivity and price when the British weren't looking. Jokes about the quality of Japanese and Taiwanese products began to stick in British throats. The technicolor hopes of the 1960s were dashed by the greyness of an oil crisis, industrial unrest, inflation at unprecedented levels and fear of Irish Republican Army (IRA) bombings. If the 1960s were symbolised by miniskirts and the mini, the 1970s were more about donkey jackets and the Austin Allegro. But it was not all bleak; Britain, under Edward Heath, were at last admitted to the EEC. And under Wilson two years later, in a referendum on whether to stay, only Shetland and the Western isles voted against, with 67 per cent of voters voting to remain. Along with membership of the EU would come an increasing internationalisation in all areas of life and freedom of movement of students, which would change the face of UK universities.

This was the era where the promise of the polytechnics as the equivalent or indeed better than the traditional universities was dashed. But even though the parity of status was not achieved, a different form of higher education institute from the universities was developed, one which had more part-time students, sandwich programmes, academic staff with industrial experience and a wider range of programmes at sub-degree level (Pratt 1997).

The polytechnics were put under local education authorities (LEA) to ensure the social control that Crosland wished. The board of governors, which often had as many as 40 members, was made up of representatives from the LEA, local industries and a few staff from the polytechnic. They had responsibility for financial planning and spending, and the academic board, which consisted of staff of the polytechnic, had complete responsibility for academic matters but no control of the funding.

The polytechnics were underfunded compared to their university counterparts in terms of overall funding per student, research funding and also non-government funding. Part of this was due to the fact that they were under the control of LEAs who often had more pressing matters to attend to in their education budgets. What local authority would suggest that a new high-tech building for the local polytechnic was a better use of money than the replacement of crumbling schools, which still had outside toilets? The polytechnic was often the largest component of the LEA's budget and the first to be squeezed. As the 1970s limped along, there was constant tension between the directors of polytechnics, who felt they had little authority, and the LEA. The LEA were in fact the employers of the staff in the polytechnics and created inflexible systems for promotion more suited to local government structures than universities. The salaries of staff in the polytechnics failed to keep up with their university counterparts and morale was low (Pratt 1997).

But for all that, they developed a distinctive higher education offering. In the student body, they were different from universities, the majority of students were from the local area, they were more mature students and part-time students, they ran different programmes, some at sub-degree level, they ran sandwich degrees and covered a different range of subjects. They were closely aligned to industry, and their staff were recruited from industry (Pratt 1997).

CHAPTER 2

BECOMING A 'REAL' UNIVERSITY –
BREAKING OF THE BINARY DIVIDE

The 1980s – big shoulder pads and even bigger hair. This was the decade when the black hole that is London began to exert its inexorable pull on the nation. The heavy industries of the North were replaced by the so-called service industries of the South, whose sole purpose, as we found out in 2008, was to serve themselves to as much of other people's money as possible.

The 1980s were about contrasts and division. Thrash Rock and New Romantics, Conservative and Socialist, haves and have nots, North and South. Greed was good, barrow boys from London's East End sold stocks and shares with the aggression and tenacity they previously flogged knocked-off perfume. Their 'loads of money', culture was lauded by the Tory government while the North was dismantled and unemployment reached new heights.

If anyone thought that the first woman prime minister would bring a more caring government, those hopes were dashed. Thatcher believed in her way or the highway, the highway being an euphemism for the hangman's noose. Playing on the arrogance of bloated trade union leaders, she quickly slipped the noose over heavy industries and trade unions who lined to put their heads in believing that they could bring down the government.

This was a woman who said that there was no such thing as society – in this woman's world it was every man for himself.

It was all meat and drink for the committee of directors of polytechnics (CDP), a group of polytechnic directors who claimed to be the voice of the whole sector – from janitors to academics. In fact, like its present-day incarnation – UK universities – it was really a pressure group lobbying for the wishes of the leaders but sold as the wishes of the whole sector.

THE 1988 EDUCATION REFORM ACT

The film *Wall Street* had just come out, with Gordon Geko, its charismatic lead character, declaring that greed was good. Desperate for a pair of red braces and the chance to be master of all it surveyed, the CDP lobbied on behalf of its members to be free from the shackles of LEAs. The members of CDP were pushing at an open door. Thatcher's hatred of the Looney Left Local Authorities – a phrase that had been coined by the *Sun* and used extensively by the Conservatives in their 1987 election campaign – was well documented, and taking away the jewel in their education department's crown – the polytechnics – was an opportunity to put them in their place – hence Part II of the 1988 Education Reform Act, where it was decided that polytechnics would be taken out of LEA control (The Education Reform Act 1988).

This gave the directors of polytechnics the chance they had been waiting for – to grab power and create a sector which encouraged manageralism, marketisation and commercialisation.

But they had to work hard for it. The initial plan for governance put forward for consultation by the department for education and science (DES) for management of polytechnics outwith LEA control was based on the same principles that Weaver had used when he set up the governance of the polytechnics in the 1960s. The intention was to allow polytechnic academic staff the same autonomy as traditional universities, where the senate traditionally had the power over all academic matters and often had significant say in all matters relating to the running of the university. Lord Annan, in a paper on governance to the committee of vice chancellors and principals (CVCP) – the universities equivalent of CDP – said that the true governing body of the university is the senate and that 'we cannot and should not want to return to the days when council really governed. We prefer government by the academic staff' (Shattock 2012b).

The vice chancellors were chairs of the senate, and in many cases considered themselves as chairmen seeking consensus rather than executives exercising authority (Jarrett 1985). To give the polytechnics a body similar to a senate, it was suggested that the new board of governors, free from LEA control, would have at least 50 per cent representation from staff and that the academic board would be responsible for academic matters and policy. The senior staff of the institution would be formed as a directorate with the director one among equals.

This was not what the directors of polytechnics wanted. The CDP formed a sub-committee, the Hatfield Group (Shattock 2012).

Their remit was to take control of the consultation and put their own interests forward above all else. For them this was not a time for wishy-washy liberal governance, rather this was the time to seize the bull by the horns and create a sector modelled on the zeitgeist of the moment. Never mind a collegiate academic organisation as proposed by the DES, what the times required was an institute modelled on the aggressive capitalism that was so admired by the press and government. And to have that you needed a dynamic leader who had total control to lead their organisation from the front and who was paid accordingly – or so those leaders thought.

The members of CDP were determined to become CEOs; they wanted to be the sole authority in their empire. They had had enough of the large boards controlled by LEAs, which many of them felt they had to wage a constant war with to get anything done.

They set about lobbying for their vision of a commercial-orientated organisation rather than a collegiate academic one, an argument that was bound to go down well with the right-wing government of the time.

One of the more prominent of the Hatfield Group, Sir Ken Green, director of Manchester Polytechnic, wrote a strong letter to the secretary of state Ken Baker to give his views of how polytechnics should be managed outwith LEA control. In his letter he railed against what he called 'Weaverism' and argued for a board similar to those which managed commercial companies, consisting mainly of representative of business and a much reduced representation from staff. He further argued against the senior management group being designated as a directorate as this would imply that they could argue against or indeed thwart the directors' wishes. All his recommendations were agreed to and the consultation became two way between the government and the directors. This saw the rise of the director of polytechnics as a CEO, unconstrained by an academic board or staff, with a board of governors who met seldom and considered the polytechnic as a business. By 1985 the committee of vice chancellors and principals (CVCP), the equivalent university body to the polytechnics CDP, could see the benefits to them of a similar system and commissioned the Jarratt report (Jarratt 1985) to look at how the management of universities could be changed to create efficiency gains. Jarratt did suggest changes in management style but kept away from anything that restricted academic autonomy or took control of academic matters away from the university staff. But over time, many post-1992 universities have adopted some of the pre-1992 management structures.

Almost immediately after the new boards were installed to govern polytechnics, the senior staff group, whose salaries were determined by these new commercial-orientated boards in remuneration committees that they sat on, saw a significant increase in salaries, company cars, health care and all the perks associated with the CEO of a multimillion pound business which had been denied them by the penny pinching LEAs (Farnham and Horton 1992). Of course, the majority of staff didn't get an increase as their salaries were not set by the board of governors.

The argument made, and still being made to this day, is that the CEOs in equivalent-sized organisations in the commercial sector were paid significantly more. And if they wanted to attract the best talent, they would have to pay a similar amount – presumably nobody on the board suggested that the existing directors may not have been the best as they had been attracted to a much smaller salary.

By the time Sir Ken, the architect of this commercial-style board, retired in 1996, he was the highest paid principal of any UK university, with a salary of £129,413 per year, 35 times more than a cleaner in his own establishment (THE 1997).

From then on, and particularly after the Dearing report in 1997 which made the boards even smaller, boards of governors of polytechnics were passive bodies dominated by their chief executive (Bennett 2002).

By 2010, Shattock wrote, 'In almost all cases of institutional difficulty – Cumbria, Gloucestershire, Leeds Metropolitan and London Metropolitan – the governing body has been found to be at fault through inaction when indicators were pointing towards trouble' (Shattock 2010). It is no coincidence that all those mentioned are post-1992 universities.

Unconstrained by the LEA and with ineffective boards, the new polytechnic directors of the late 1980s followed the business model that was prevalent at the time. 'Have a dispute with your staff and crush the unions' was the order of the day.

Successive governments had been committed to massification of higher education and there was a widely agreed goal to have 30 per cent of young people in higher education.

When the polytechnics were taken out of LEA control, the funding bodies, first the National Advisory Board for Public Sector Higher Education (NAB) then the Polytechnics and Colleges Funding Council (PCFC), had realised that funding was the simplest and the most direct way that they could exert some sort of control over polytechnics. They moved away from historic funding to targets. As Pratt (1997) says, through bodies such as 'NAB, and subsequently PCFC, government could direct the polytechnics and other institutions towards particular kinds of provision and to dramatically increase efficiency'.

By providing more income for certain subjects or quotas in others, they could try to ensure that polytechnics were providing programmes in areas where the government felt there was a need rather than expanding in subjects where there was student demand. However, this was not entirely efficient at a local level. The funding was not tailored to individual polytechnics, regions or cities. Rather it was based on national needs.

A national-level market was developed where institutions had to compete with one another for quotas and income. They did so with a vengeance. This resulted in a bidding war where the more aggressive institutes, who wanted to increase in size, lowered their fees causing a lowering of fees and unit cost throughout the sector. In sharp contrast, universities that had a similar bidding process formed a cartel in the subsequent year and ensured that their unit of funding – the amount of funding per student – would not decrease at the same rate (Pratt 1997).

But for the sector, the result was that in 1989, with a 15 per cent participation rate in higher education, the funding from government per full-time equivalent (FTE) in higher education was at an all-time high of £9,530. By 1992, with the polytechnics becoming universities and the reclassification of many students who were in Higher National Diploma and Higher National Certificate programmes as higher education, there was 23 per cent participation but the government funding per FTE dropped to £6,245 (Wyness 2010).

The only way to manage this decrease in funding was through efficiency gains. In 1989, the polytechnics, who were now the employers rather than the LEA, tabled a new contract to manage an increase in student numbers, which had not come with an increase in funding.

They radically altered the conditions of employment for academic staff, which the teacher unions claimed increased the required hours of lecturers by 25 per cent and the number of working weeks in a year by 20 per cent. There followed three years of varying levels of industrial action until agreement on the new contract was finally reached in 1992. For a relatively small salary increase the majority of academic staff moved to the new contract and gave up much of their holiday entitlement and agreed to increased teaching hours

Since this industrial unrest, the nature of the relationship between the senior management and staff had changed forever. Formerly, both sides agreed that the problems with salaries and contracts were imposed on them by their employers, the LEAs, but not now. Now with senior staff receiving significant year-on-year increases in salaries unrelated to the salaries of the rest of the staff, a 'them and us' attitude developed in employee relations.

But the new contract wasn't enough; staff in the polytechnics had to work out how they would manage to teach this new influx of students. In the 1970s, staff to student ratios had held steady at 7:1 but by the time the polytechnics were made into universities, it was 17.2:1 (Pratt 1997).

Programmes were modularised and academic staff redesigned learning to reduce contact hours. This was all carried out under the banner of student-centred learning, which had long been recognised as a valid method of ensuring engagement with learning. However, nowhere in the writings about the value of student-centred learning to individual learners had it been promoted as a more efficient way of using a decreasing resource base. In fact, to create an environment where the learning experience is personalised is resource-intensive – especially with the learning technology that was available in the 1980s.

Only 24 per cent of the academic staff in polytechnics had teaching qualifications in the late 1980s (Pratt 1997) and most of those were found in the polytechnic departments of education which had formerly been colleges of education before they were amalgamated into the polytechnics.

In 1989, Her Majesty's Inspectorate (HMI) looked at staff development in polytechnics and found that while there was significant engagement, the majority was focused on attainment of further qualifications and only 12 per cent on improving teaching skills. In the late 1980s it was not unusual for the only teacher training a new academic member of staff would get was to spend a few weeks shadowing an existing lecturer – usually the lecturer being shadowed did not have a teaching qualification. This did not mean that teaching was not of a high level. An HMI (1989) report concluded that in most institutions, and in most courses, there was evidence of outstanding teaching and only 10 to 20 per cent of teaching would be considered poor.

However, while outstanding, it was not necessarily innovative. In vocational subjects where the teachers had many years industrial experience, it was its relevance and evidence of engagement with the real world that was the main feature of polytechnic teaching and which differentiated it from university teaching. At no time did HMI suggest that, in order to improve teaching, staff should look at new theories of education that suggested they should have less contact with students.

So the notion that in the late 1980s the aging cohort of lecturers, as described in an HMI report in 1984 (HMI, Engineering in polytechnics: 1984), teaching practical subjects such as engineering, applied sciences and accountancy embraced student-centred learning with a zeal that transformed all programmes in the polytechnic is highly unlikely. The thought that polytechnic academic staff were suddenly steeped in the works of Dewy, Piaget and Vygotsky, and sat about discussing the zone of proximal development and epistemic cognition and, from this deep understanding of pedagogue, changed the previous system of teaching to student-centred learning is of course not what happened.

The brutal truth is that it was from necessity rather than pedagogue that polytechnics redesigned their programmes to have less contact hours. They did not have enough staff to cover the new intakes. It was only after this fact that it was called student-centred, self-deterministic, self-directed, or any other such name to claim an academic justification that was not warranted.

In the National Committee Inquiry Into Higher Education 1997 chaired by Ronald Dearing, the former head of the post office, Dearing stated that his survey of providers showed that 'a large number of academics' have had no training in, for example, the 'use of information technology for learning and teaching'. He went on to say that 'A number of those offering us evidence commented on the irony that, in institutions devoted to learning and teaching and to the advancement of knowledge and understanding, so little attention is paid to equipping staff with advanced knowledge and understanding of the processes of learning and teaching. Many see a need to rectify this situation'. His report went on to say that staff saw that promotion opportunities were related to research and long service rather than teaching (Dearing 1997).

The report noted that by 1997, 'The learning environment of students today is quite unlike that in the 1960s. The dramatic increase in student numbers, which has not been matched by a proportionate increase in funding, staffing or other resources, has resulted in increased class sizes, decreased class contact time for students, and an increase in students studying off campus' (Dearing 1997).

Lea et al. (2003, 4) identified one of the issues with student-centred learning as the fact that 'many institutions or educators claim to be putting student-centred learning into practice, but in reality they are not'.

In a comparative analysis of English higher education and European higher education in 2009 (HEFC 2009), it was concluded that English degrees are shorter than European equivalents, class contact was less and the amount of effort that students needed to expend to gain a degree was less. The research showed that in almost all subjects studied, students in post-1992 universities spent less time studying than pre-1992 university students. Worryingly, these differences applied to contact time as well as private study, belying the notion that because students in post-1992 universities tend to have weaker academic ability they receive more intensive teaching than pre-1992 university students.

But the deceit that polytechnics and then post-1992 universities were leaders in student-centred learning, which promoted creative graduates, was promulgated to hide this fact and still continues to this day.

This vision of a system which developed creative graduates ready for the modern world became the main selling point of UK universities all over the world, and for the most part it was believed. Not many bothered to take a look to see if the emperor really had any clothes.

Living off the status of a few world-class universities, post-1992 universities sold their modular undergraduate degree system running over only three years (four in Scotland) with contact hours of less than 14 hours throughout the world.

But more than that, the idea that academics could and should be flexible and creative around programme design to meet financial and resource imperatives was embedded in the DNA of ex-polytechnics. This flexibility and adaptability became one of the defining features of post-1992 universities and allowed them to win so-called market share overseas, even in competition with what the British Council called aggressive tactics from the likes of Australian universities.

THE 1992 ACT

Perhaps it was after having a Currie for lunch – Edwina, that is, that John Major, the UK prime minister, reportedly asked the department of education to find something that would be cheap and popular for him to do in his first term. He had already begun the abolition of the poll tax and wanted to keep on a roll. Ken Clarke, Major's first education secretary, responded with a letter looking at long-term issues in education, and in a section on higher education, he suggested that getting rid of the binary divide would fulfill both criteria. It was strong argument (Ratcliffe 2018).

John Major was unusual for a UK prime minister; he had not attended any higher education, let alone Oxbridge.

The CDP had long argued that the binary divide was an example of British class elitism, with the polytechnics, whose students were generally more working class, having less funding. So here was a way to create the classless society that Major advocated and make education fairer.

So it wasn't surprising that one and a half years later, by the time of the next general election, not only the Conservatives but also Labour and the other political parties had put the abolition of the binary divide in their manifesto.

In reality, it was the differing response to expansion from the late 1980s that was the impetus for the unification. Given how polytechnic directors had embraced the notion of massification of higher education in a way that the universities had failed to do, Clarke decided to put the cat among the pigeons by making them part of the university sector. Universities were not achieving the efficiency goals and increase in numbers that the government wanted. Abolishing the binary line was seen as a means of facilitating greater competition between institutions and ensuring expansion at reduced costs.

In his letter to the prime minister, Clarke argued for a single funding council (thus breaking the binary divide). He stated, 'The natural evolution of the reforms for Higher Education contained in the 1988 Act is to bring together the two Higher Education sectors – Universities, and Polytechnics and Colleges – under a single Funding Council. That will ensure that the system can continue to expand cost-effectively and without artificial barriers' (Ratcliffe 2018).

He further argued for the polytechnics to be allowed to use the title university, but warned that financial drivers would have to be used to maintain the distinctive nature of polytechnics.

This was something that Major was at pains to ensure. A letter to Ken Clarke from the prime minister's office specifically asked for assurances that the proposal would not allow for the polytechnics to shift their course, mix or research programmes to favour more academic subjects (Ratcliffe 2018).

Clarke wrote back claiming that the polytechnics' directors had already made it clear that they 'would not want to change their present missions for teaching and research should they be allowed to adopt university title and status' (Ratcliffe 2018).

At that time Clarke argued that a shift to more academic subjects would not happen. Due to 'student-related funding arrangements' (Ratcliffe 2018).

But the directors of polytechnics had other views about social control through 'student-related funding'. Many believed that having a different mission would retain a form of the binary divide and could never deliver comparability of status or funding and that the only way to achieve this was to become a university. And this couldn't just be in name. In order to get maximum benefit from the change of status, they had to become indistinguishable from the existing universities. The 1992 Act allowed 38 polytechnics/colleges to become universities immediately, with another 51 to follow soon after. Polytechnics and large higher education colleges were awarded royal charters that gave them full autonomy with degree-awarding powers and the right to use the title of university.

It was the final act in the academic drift that successive governments had claimed they wanted to avoid. Although many hoped that this meant that vocational qualifications had now been granted acknowledgement and the same status as purely academic ones. And what was seen by some as a formalised class system was finished.

CHAPTER 3

MONEY MATTERS

ROBBING UNIVERSITIES

From the early years, capital expenditure on polytechnics was less than universities. In 1972–73 the polytechnics received £6 million in government funding and universities £28 million. The university sector was bigger at the time, but even accounting for this, the capital expenditure per place was £10,700 in universities as opposed to £7,500 in polytechnics (Lewis 1974), and that was new spend. Given that most universities had historic assets which generated funding on top of government funding, in the words of Lewis, the polytechnics were not so much 'different from and equal to' as 'different from and poorer'.

In 1987–88, by the time polytechnics were taken out of LEA control, universities' capital funding was three times that of polytechnics (Pratt 1997). Recurrent funding was also unequal between polytechnics and universities with spend on universities staying at four times that of polytechnics almost the whole period of their existence

It terms of non-exchequer income, there was a disparity as well. The breaking away of polytechnics from LEAs had intended to encourage them to be more entrepreneurial as they were now allowed to keep any surpluses they could generate. This was the beginning of polytechnics and then new universities trying to build internal business. But by the time they received their charter, income from industry accounted for only 2 per cent of income in the polytechnics but 6.3 per cent of a much larger income in the universities. Externally funded research accounted for 2 per cent in polytechnics but 20 per cent in universities (Lewis 1974).

So it was no surprise that when the polytechnic and colleges funding council (PCFC) was established to take over the management of funding, in the short time between the Education Reform Act and polytechnics gaining university status, it found that the polytechnics estate was in a bad state. It was estimated that some £75 million would be needed to make urgent repairs just to comply with legal requirements (Pratt 1997).

When the sectors merged and polytechnics became universities, the directors of polytechnics felt that they would get a fair share of the funding from the newly merged higher education funding council including research funding. But it was not to be.

The new university directors had already had their outstretched fingers burnt in the PCFC bidding war that they had engaged wholeheartedly in. The last round before unification in 1992, had created a 16 per cent increase in numbers with a 13 per cent increase in funds (Wyness 2010).

But by then they weren't worried, as they were giddy with the success of becoming universities. They assumed that they would be involved in a new funding process in a common funding council, which would reallocate funds from the old universities to them and allow them to achieve parity with their new university colleagues.

The CDP were going to undertake a Robin Hood strategy they gloated out loud (Pratt 1997). But they were naive. Although the universities had agreed to accept a common funding council, it didn't mean they were going to give away any of their cash to the new upstarts. CDP argued for a funding regime based on an idea of 'efficient expansion' (Pratt 1997, 236). The plan was to use the notion of efficiency to benefit the cheaper polytechnics over the more expensive universities. What followed after the polytechnics gaining university status was a year of the old universities developing a new narrative through the soon to be abolished, university funding council. The argument was developed that funding for university students was not actually much different from that of polytechnic students in terms of fees. In the 1980s, after adjustments for research, the department of education and science (DES) found the cost to teach an arts student in university was 20 per cent higher than in polytechnics. But by 1992 miraculously, with many more so-called adjustments, the university funding council, just before it was amalgamated into the new joint higher education funding council for England (HEFCE), argued that the difference was minimal. They showed that although universities may receive more money, they were still as efficient as the polytechnics – after adjustments of course – and so should still receive the same higher level of funding. The same argument was used in Scotland. That general principal was accepted.

The new joint funding council HEFCE opted for a model that gave core funding for existing places at much the same level as had been funded before with an efficiency gain and extra funds at different fee levels for different subjects and for high-cost institutions. So the only way that the new universities could gain more income was, as before, by expanding in areas that the government funded at a higher level. Yet again, while the ex-polytechnics jumped at the chance to expand, the pre-1992 universities were more cautious – which proved to be wise, because soon after the expansion came consolidation – a process far harder to manage.

RESEARCH INCOME

In terms of research income, the new universities engaged in a lengthy administrative process that was rigged against them – time and time again. The research assessment exercise (RAE) was used as a way of determining the quality of research conducted and for allocating funding. In 1992, post-1992 universities were involved for the first time the RAE continued every four years until 2008 when it was replaced with the research excellence framework (REF), which has run once in 2014.

The RAE in 1992 allowed institutes to decide which research-active staff they wished to include in their submission to the exercise. A total of 192 universities entered the RAE with some 43,000 researchers entered.

Post-1992 universities waited with bated breath as the panels, which consisted almost entirely of eminent researchers from traditional universities, decided on the worthiness of the research that the post-1992 universities had been carrying out on a shoestring. The traditional universities received 91 per cent of available funding with post-1992 universities receiving 7 per cent and colleges the remaining 2 per cent. Some results were challenged in courts and judges ruled that the system should be more transparent. What was transparently obvious was those that had the money had no intention of letting anyone else get it. By 2008 there had been a number of tweaks to make it fairer– but only for the elite. By 2008–2009, 90 per cent of the funding went to 38 universities (Pace 2018). Subsequent changes increased this number to 48 universities but there was no doubt post-1992 universities were not suddenly, or ever, awash with research funding.

But in most post-1992 universities research is still prized above all other academic activities with staff being measured by their results in the REF. Many post-1992 universities nowadays stipulate that an essential criteria for a teaching post is a PhD and research background rather than industrial experience that had been prized as polytechnics.

For many staff in post-1992 universities, the effort of being involved in RAE/ REF exercises is onerous as it involves a significant workload and it is highly unlikely to result in substantial funding. In fact Rama Thirunamachandran, director of research, innovation and skills at HEFCE between 2002 and 2008 tried to cut the workload associated with the ever-expanding RAE – which, by then, had become a major concern – but he was not successful. A review he carried out with Sir Gareth Roberts in 2003 proposed an institutional opt-out for teaching-focused institutions in return for a base level of funding to sustain research capacity. However, this was rejected by the post-1992 institutions, who would have benefited by this and to this day all involve themselves in research assessment exercises (Jump 2013).

The argument is that to opt out of the RAE would develop a new binary system, with the old polytechnics in effect becoming second-class citizens as teaching-intensive institutions.

So, despite the fact that they are unlikely to receive any funding, post-1992 universities contribute their bit to the costly research assessment exercises – the treasury estimated in 2008 that it cost £47 million across English universities to submit in the REF (Jump 2013). Looking at the REF for 2014, it is clear that post-1992 universities do little research that is considered by the REF. Typically a large post-1992 university may submit 100–200 staff on an average of 11 areas whereas a similar-sized research-intensive university will submit over a thousand staff across almost all 36 units of assessment. Despite this, many ex-polytechnics feel that it is essential to have a significant research presence and income to be able to be seen as a real university and to compete for funding.

However, this is a choice that they have made to try to join the club and emulate the traditional universities rather than take the hint and form a club of their own. Where research is not the measure of success and qualifications are not so much research informed as useful and practical.

NEED FOR NEW FUNDING SOURCES

It was apparent to the new universities that to be equal to pre-1992 universities, they needed to make up the gap in funding. No amount of efficiency gains would allow for that, and so commercialisation was the only answer.

Since Thatcher had introduced full fees for overseas students, pre-1992 universities and polytechnics had been actively recruiting overseas with some success – 16 per cent of pre-1992 students were international as opposed to 6 per cent of ex-polytechnic students. Many believed that a change in name and status of the university would make it easier to attract international students.

It took some ex-polytechnics longer than others to realise that this was where the pot of gold was. But when they did, as we will see in the following chapters, they changed the face of international recruitment, making it more commercial and cutthroat. This was inevitable as they had a harder sell and a greater need for the fee income than the majority of pre-1992 universities.

Encouraged by the government and given a free reign by weak governance, post-1992 universities led the way in the UK for a race to the bottom – accepting students not so much on academic merit as commercial potential.

The success of their tactics to develop these new paying markets meant that the new universities could develop in ways which had little to do with UK's national interests and training needs. The influx of funding from overseas students and overseas market demand for particular programmes meant that the makeup of the graduates and qualifications offered in ex-polytechnics was by its definition no longer related to local or even national needs. It was a direct result of the reliance on overseas income and related to the needs of the larger markets in the world. The shape and size of new universities was determined by strategic decisions based on institutional greed rather than national need.

CHAPTER 4

UK PRIME MINISTER'S
INITIATIVE (PMI)

Tony Blair, when fighting for re-election in 2001, wrote in the Labour manifesto that the Labour Party's top priority 'is and always will be education, education, education'. After all, an educated population would have understood why he needed to invade Iraq without him having to lie about weapons of mass destruction (WMDs) and that would have made life just so much easier. While his statement was primarily about schools, in his manifesto he set out a target to have 50 per cent per cent of school leavers in some form of higher education (Labour Party 2001). A big ambition, but how was he going to pay for it?

Just four years earlier, when he first entered Number 10, he had inherited the outgoing Conservative government's Dearing Report, which had been commissioned before the general election. The Dearing Report, 'Higher Education in the Learning Society', was given the remit to make recommendations on 'the purpose, shape, structure, size and funding of Higher Education over the next twenty years'. Dearing suggested an increase in participation to around 45 per cent (in 1997 at the time of the report, participation rates were on average around 30 per cent with 45 per cent already achieved in Northern Ireland and Scotland). At the beginning of the report, Dearing mentioned that public funding in higher education had fallen by 40 per cent since 1976. He argued that with a further increased participation rate, there would be a significant shortfall. And that 'We are convinced that the gap is real and cannot be closed simply by further efficiency savings on the part of institutions'. The report concluded that 'Graduates in employment should make a greater contribution to Higher Education in the future' (Dearing 1997). This heralded the Blair government's introduction of a £1,000 graduate fee with means testing which would ensure that the poorest one-third of students would pay nothing. Many Labour voters saw any fee for higher education as a betrayal of socialist principals.

Dearing pointed out that a graduate fee system at that rate would not fully fill the gap in funding, which he estimated would have been £2 billion a year by 2017 – without any extra funding put into the system.

In the report, Dearing pointed out that 'The objective for higher education must be to develop diverse sources of funding so that it has the flexibility to adapt to changing circumstances' (Dearing 1997).

Blair was well aware that with an absolute cap on fees of £1,000 he had promised, the gap was looming and he saw a way to help close it without dipping into government funds.

By the late 1990s the numbers of globally mobile students had risen from a few elite to over 1.7 million, and as particularly Asian countries became richer, the trend was upwards. It wasn't hard to predict this increase, as UK universities had been actively increasing the numbers of full-fee-paying students that they attracted. By 1997 there were 116,840 non-EU international students in tertiary education in the UK (HESA n.d.).

Tony Blair launched the first phase of his Prime Minister's Initiative for Attracting Overseas Students (PMI) to encourage UK universities to attract even more fee-paying overseas students. The aim was to increase the numbers of international students in UK higher education by 50,000 over six years (The National Archives 1999). PMI was to be funded by the government and education institutes to the tune of over £40 million. Blair pulled together a number of departments (Education and Employment, Trade and Industry, Foreign and Commonwealth Office, the Devolved Assemblies of Scotland and Wales and the Department of Defence) to manage the initiative.

PMI was not about helping others, it was not about the long- or even medium-term gain. It was about making a quick buck in the market place. There were no real plans to give assistance to developing countries and create sustainable equal partnerships, no investment in infrastructure, no significant money flowing out of the country to those in need.

No, of course not. This was Tony Blair's government – where spin was king.

EDUCATION@UK

To kick-start the first PMI, the British Council commissioned market research to find out the perceived strengths and weakness of UK higher education. The Brand Report BC (British Council 1999, 1) was the outcome of this research. The Brand Report sought to compare perceptions of UK higher education in comparison to its 'competitors', especially Australia and the United States, and concluded that the UK was seen as elite and high quality, but also as expensive, less friendly than Australia, and less innovative than the United States.

From this was developed an overarching brand for the UK higher education sector. Only 30 years before, Robbins had written that there was no coherent higher education sector in the UK and there were only 22 or so universities at that time.

But in the 1990s and early 2000, the British Council developed a brand for a sector that encompassed a hundred or so institutions of differing age, provenance, funding, traditions and quality.

The remit was to develop an umbrella identity to differentiate UK's education offering from its competitors like Australia and the United States.

Universities with world-class reputations and hundreds of years of traditions, with alumni that had won Noble Prizes, Fields Medals, or invented the World Wide Web were lumped together with post-1992 wannabes.

All came together as Education@UK – 'a dynamic tradition; the new world class; being the best I can be' and was 'responsive; welcoming; alive with possibilities'. A panacea, all things to all people, and according to the Brand, it covered every university in the land. Not bad for a sector chronically underfunded by successive governments (British Council 1999).

The Brand was to be managed by the British Council, which developed visual identities, logos, advice for institutions on marketing, a database of education agents and promotional materials for institutions to use alongside their own materials.

Within three years of the PMI being introduced, the UK saw an increase in international student numbers of 91 per cent. By 2005 the targets had been exceeded by 43,000 in both higher education and further education (FE). Tony Blair claimed this as a success even though over the same period the UK had lost 3 per cent of its market share (Böhm et al. 2004). Perhaps a better measure of success was that a number of countries imitated the work done by Education@ UK brand.

But there was an unexpected legacy. By creating a brand rather than a strategy, the PMI extended the commercial language of marketing to education.

Before the PMI there had been much debate about education being run as an industry rather than a public service. Frequent letters to the editors of the quality press or opinion pieces in trade papers rallied against the increased use of economic arguments in the development of academic strategies in universities.

But PMI blew the debate out of the water. PMI was all about selling, not about teaching or service to society. Programmes and courses became products, countries became markets. Endorsed by the Labour government, encouraged by the press and media, in UK higher education, almost uniquely in Europe, the language of trade had taken over. And from language comes a culture. There was no stipulation that universities should put some of the fees aside to give scholarships for clever poor students or to assist the countries they were working in. There were no guidelines to ensure that young people and families investing their life savings would get unbiased advice and assistance to ensure that they enrolled in the most appropriate programme and university for them. No discussion on which countries they should work in and which they shouldn't. International students had already been reduced to targets by many UK universities but PMI declared open season on them.

The UK embraced the notion of higher education as a trade with an enthusiasm equalled only by the Australians.

VISION 2020

By 2004, according to the prime minister, PMI had been successful. There had been a larger than expected increase in absolute numbers of international students studying in the UK although this represented a decrease in market share. The funding for PMI was running out in 2005 and the British Council was very keen to find evidence to persuade the government to continue investing and supporting international education. They needed to persuade the government that a further PMI was likely to continue to have positive results.

To do this, the British Council published Vision 2020 Forecasting International Student Mobility a UK Perspective (Bohm et al. 2004). Freed from the shackles of peer review, the academics who compiled this report put forward a biased view of the increase in international students the UK higher education sector could expect. It wasn't necessarily the academic rigour of the research, as the bias of the reporting of the research, that could be called into question.

The report presented research into the future demand for UK higher education over the period 2003 to 2020, some 17 years. One may ask, why chose 17 years? Was there something specific that would happen in 17 years' time?

Who in 2003 would have predicted the collapse of the world banking system in 2008, the effect of social media on perceptions, Facebook, Twitter and Skype – which were only starting – the Arab Spring uprisings in 2011, US invasion of Iraq, the 7/7 bombs in London, the launch of the iPad, smart phones and so on.

However, if you want to have some really big potential headline figures to go along with your snappy title the longer period you forecast over the bigger.

Vision 2020 a perfect vision of the future, clear, no need for lenses. But it was through lenses, rose-tinted ones, that the report was compiled.

The report was published by the British Council and IDP Australia. IDP carried out similar functions for Australian universities that the British Council carried out for UK universities. Both had a vested interest in encouraging increased investment in international education.

It employed a model that allowed the forecasting of global demand for international student places from 144 countries through forecasting over the period 2003–20. The model provided forecasts of demand for international student places for individual destination countries and grouped them into regions.

As well as an estimate of potential overall demand for international education throughout the world to 2020, Vision 2020 attempted to measure the relative attractiveness of the UK compared to the other main English-speaking destinations (MESD) – United States, Canada, Australia and New Zealand. Is Katie Price more attractive than Kim Kardashian?

From this, Vision 2020 developed three scenarios. A pessimistic scenario where the UK lost market share, particularly due to a loss of attractiveness because of a decline in quality, a base scenario where it maintained the same market share and an optimistic scenario where the UK gained market share.

It is no surprise, given who the authors of the report were, that the summary of the main implications at the beginning of the report comes straight from the optimistic scenario. It starts with, 'The study forecasts that UK higher education may experience a tripling of the current level of demand for international students to 850,000 by 2020. Similarly, for programmes delivered through a variety of arrangements transnationally, growth is forecast to increase rapidly – from the current figure of approximately 190,000 students to over 800,000 by 2020' (Bohm et al. 2004).

In the whole 90-page document, there is only one short section and one graph with a forecast of the number of international students that could be expected in 2020 in the pessimistic scenario and that still forecasts growth over the period.

There are, however, numerous tables and charts showing and comparing the optimistic and the base scenario where the pessimistic scenario is left out completely.

To be fair, they also run a forecast with a price escalation scenario for the UK. But in the British Council model, an increase in prices of UK education gives a perception of higher quality, and attractiveness goes up – as does the numbers of students. The model predicts that if UK higher education costs escalated, the UK would have increased its share of the world market from 23 per cent to 36 per cent! What this price escalation modelling shows is that the British Council was out of touch with the realities and challenges that post-1992 universities – who often had to discount fees heavily – were faced with when marketing themselves overseas.

Whether the British Council wished to paint a rosy picture of the potential for universities to increase numbers over the following 17 years or not, the hard facts were obvious.

Barring some worldwide catastrophe, there was almost certainly going to be a continuing increase in demand for higher education for international students overall.

The forecast of overall demand for international student places was firmly based on the predicted increase in populations, increase in wealth and some measures of whether the host country would or could meet this demand. These were based on much more precise data than any measure of attractiveness. It was forecast that 'Overall, the model projects the total global demand for international student places to increase from about 2.1 million in 2003 to 3.3 million in 2010 and approximately 5.8 million in 2020' (British Council 1999, 4).

This actually proved to be a conservative estimate, as by 2009 the actual number of globally mobile students in the world was 3.5 million (IHE Report 2009) as opposed to the forecast 3.3 million.

But in contrast, the estimate of numbers that would study in the UK was significantly exaggerated. By 2016–17 the total number of international students in UK higher education was nowhere near the much-vaunted 850,000 expected by 2020 or even the base-line scenario of 511,00. The reality was that by 2016–17, there were only 450,000 international students in UK higher education and this number is declining (HESA 2018). Also, with Brexit, this decline might become a drop. There were 138,000 EU students studying in the UK in 2017–18. Regulations dictate that they have to be treated, in terms of fees, as UK citizens and so have access to UK government loans for fees. Should this not continue and EU students become liable for upfront international fees, it is likely to destroy this market. While it would be unfair to expect the authors of Vision 2020 to have predicted Brexit, it shows the hubris involved in forecasting over such a long period.

Vision 2020 was accepted by all in the international education scene as gospel. It unleashed a wave of expansion in international offices, faculties, directorates based on the Word according to the British Council. International strategies in universities across the land opened with the immortal line from

Vision 2020, 'The study forecasts that UK higher education may experience a tripling of the current level of demand for international students to 850,000 by 2020.'

Expansion was the order of the day as universities scrambled to make sure they would get their slice of the over-egged cake.

BROADENING OUR HORIZONS

Not to be outdone by the British Council, universities through their representative bodies also wanted to influence the prime minister to continue funding their international activities and to continue to fund the British Council offices overseas, which were considered to be excellent.

So in 2004, UKCISA, the UK Council for International Student Affairs – a membership body which in 2004 included all UK universities and called itself a 'a national advisory body serving the interests of international students in the UK and those who work with them', published a survey in association with the British Council, universities of UK and the Standing Committee of Principals. Taken with Vision 2020, this was an attempt to suggest how, universities could make themselves more attractive to foreign students so as to create the environment for the Vision 2020 optimistic scenario so loved by all finance directors.

The survey 'International Students in UK universities and colleges. Broadening Our Horizons' (UKCISA 2004, 14) was the first attempt to look at international student experience since the Heist survey of 1994. The report points out that because of the focus on international students as a market, 'much research has focused on students' decision-making process prior to coming to the UK, but there has been no large-scale study of international students' experiences and perceptions after arrival'.

But Broadening Our Horizons is still based on the notion of international students as a cash generator and the international student as a customer. It is in fact a customer satisfaction survey and firmly intended to be used to help institutions recruit more international students rather than improve the lot of the whole student body, let alone help internationalise home students.

The report relied on students filling in a survey, and post-1992 universities were underrepresented. Of 80,000 international students in post-1992 universities in 2004 (HESA n.d.) only 757 students responded (0.9 per cent) as compared to 3,529 pre-1992 students who responded from an overall population of 166,000 (2 per cent). In most cases the survey reflected the geographic makeup of international students in the sector with the highest number of respondents,

889, being from China, which at the time was the largest provider of students to the UK at 31,930. However, Greece, the second largest provider of students at 24,280, only had 192 respondents. The experience of Greek students may have been particularly interesting, as they had been the largest provider of students for a number of years with 27,950 students in 1998 at a time when China only provided 3,850.

MARKETING

As well as being a customer satisfaction survey, Broadening Our Horizons was an admission that a significant proportion of UK universities were selling themselves and their programmes too hard and were unable to deliver on their promises.

For much of the report, it is hard to differentiate between post-1992 universities and pre-1992 universities, but where one can do so, it is clear that post-1992 universities were the biggest culprits.

The preface to the report says,

> We must not take for granted that UK education offers international students a good 'product', or concentrate only on 'selling'. If we are to continue recruiting international students successfully then the experience has to compare favourably to the expectation generated by the promotion, whether that promotion is undertaken at a national level by the Education@UK brand, or at a local level by individual institutions.

> Now that the PMI is coming to the end of its first phase and the impact and future development of the Education UK brand is being considered, it is timely for us to turn the spotlight on the level of satisfaction with the student experience, to see whether it does match up to what the marketing now claims, and whether promotional materials reflect the reality. (UKCISA 2004, 14)

This is hardly surprising because throughout the period of PMI, as universities increasingly treated international student recruitment as a commercial operation, they had begun to develop sophisticated marketing materials. This was particularly true of universities who had little by way of a world-wide brand.

Many post-1992 universities were housed in cities where there had been large-scale manufacturing employers who needed skilled staff. The collapse of

Britain's industrial and manufacturing economy left many inner cities blighted with unemployment riddled with poor housing and socially excluded from more prosperous suburban districts. Most traditional universities could sell themselves on the strengths of their research, past alumni and position in world league tables. This was not the case for post-1992 universities and a few less attractive older universities.

To counter this, these universities developed exquisitely tailored messages that highlighted the best points of studying in their university and town and ignore the bad.

To this day smiling faces of students on green fields or hills with blue skies, ancient castles, attractive young girls in lab coats holding test tubes or looking at shiny expensive machinery adorn glossy prospectuses and web sites. The world of these fictional students is always sunny.

VALUE FOR MONEY

The report (UKCISA 2004) showed a high level of satisfaction with students' time in the UK but highlighted a number of areas for concern, in particular, around finance, accommodation and integration with UK students. The survey reported that many students saw themselves as 'cash cows' and only 47 per cent of non-EU students were satisfied with the value of their course with that dropping lower for Chinese and Asian students. In all, 72 per cent had found the cost of living higher than they had been given to expect.

Where differentiation was shown between post- and pre-1992 universities, it would seem that students who joined post-1992 universities were in general less well qualified, had poorer English and were from poorer economic backgrounds (UKCISA 2004). In accommodation, students who used university accommodation were most satisfied; 90 per cent of undergraduates in pre-1992 universities were offered accommodation and only 72 per cent in post-1992 universities.

DISCOUNTS

In the open market, low ranked, post-1992 universities in little-known cities have few ways of differentiating themselves. Most use discounts, which they called scholarships, to reduce fees. In many countries these are available to every student. They allow poorer students to afford the fees but this also means that many of them have to work to be able to afford to live in the UK.

The report notes:

> It is sometimes a concern to UK institutions that international students who receive part-scholarships are tempted to take these up without making adequate arrangements to finance the remaining costs. (UKCISA 2004, 50)

It is no surprise that in the report, students in post-1992 universities were more likely to report financial hardship and to look for part-time work. But according to the report, post-1992 university students found it harder to get work. Given that most part-time work that students take is not related to their studies, it is unlikely that this shows a bias from bars and burger joints to employ students from better-ranked universities. It is more likely to reflect the fact that these students had poorer English levels or were studying in areas of higher indigenous unemployment.

Many overseas students from academic systems with extensive class contact found it strange to find class contact often only for three days a week and only 14 hours a week. Over two 15-week semesters of which only 11 were designated teaching weeks, all for a bargain basement price of £10,000 plus living expenses of a similar amount. In student feedback obtained under PMI2 research for the Brand, many questioned whether they were getting value for money.

ACADEMIC REQUIREMENTS

Throughout the UK university sector, academics had to wrestle with a whole cohort of students used to different forms of interaction with academic staff and different ways of studying who found the more interactive hands-off approach of UK academic life more challenging than expected.

Post-1992 universities were actually better placed to deal with these differences, as they had experience of academic culture shock and how to manage it. Over the late 1990s and early 2000s, post-1992 universities had redesigned their programmes to allow for non-standard entry requirements and more advanced entry students from diplomas in the UK. They argued that the first two years of a higher national diploma (HND) were the same level of study as the first two of a degree and so it was unfair if students had to effectively repeat a year or even two by being admitted into first or second year of an undergraduate degree.

Traditional universities took the view that the learning experience in a HND was substantially different from the first two years of their degrees, with university degrees being more theoretical from the start than diplomas and so they were less flexible with their entry requirements. They were rejecting large numbers of students already, and it was always easier for planning purposes to know that you had a student for three or four years than try to balance the quota with a large volume of final year entries.

Post-1992 universities did not have that luxury; thus they had a great deal of experience in helping UK students, who would be considered to be less academic, to manage the transition to university and they used this experience to allow them to adopt 'flexible' international entry criteria. They allowed international students with a wide range of academic experience into programmes.

This meant that post-1992 universities needed to develop pre-sessional programmes to address the academic differences and language shortcomings of large bodies of students, particularly from China.

These involved intensive English language programmes and also programmes intended to help students adapt to a different educational culture, understand about plagiarism and the fact that they had almost no classes to attend. Many pre-1992 universities had similar programmes but their students were stronger academically.

So it is no surprise that the report found that students in post-1992 universities were more likely to attend orientation events, make more use of support services and attend language and study classes.

CHAPTER 5

PRIME MINISTER'S INITIATIVE FOR INTERNATIONAL EDUCATION (PMI2)

The carrots were dangled. Vision 2020 (Bohm et al. 2004) guaranteeing success of another PMI – even if market share plummeted, there would still be an increase in numbers – according to the forecasts of the British Council. And there was even a report, Broadening Our Horizons (UKCISA 2004), to tell the prime minister where to spend the money to ensure even more success –a perfect example of how academics who scent funding can put together compelling proposal.

But at the time it wasn't all plain sailing; there was an increasing backlash against immigration from the eight formerly East European countries that joined the EU in 2004.

In the 2004 European elections the until-then marginalised UK Independence Party (UKIP) won 2.6 million votes, 16.1 per cent of the vote, coming in third with 12 members of the European Parliament (MEPs). During the campaign, UKIP highlighted immigration from East European countries as an issue for working-class Brits. Many who would be entitled to immigrate would do so to study under the freedom-of-movement rules. This also includes the fact that EU citizens had to be charged the same fees as home citizens rather than the overseas fee.

The UK could have put initial restrictions on the number of immigrants allowed in from the new accession states. But, along with only Ireland and Sweden, the UK decided not to do so. All other pre-2004 countries put in place some temporary employment and movement restrictions.

By the time the A2 countries, Bulgaria and Romania, had joined the EU in 2007, the UK did place restrictions, including restrictions on the right to higher education, reflecting a change in the government's view of immigration and the start of the move away from internationalisation and globalisation and towards the eventual Brexit referendum.

In April 2006, egged on by the heady view of a tripling market as reported in Vision 2020, Blair launched the Prime Minister's Initiative for International Education (PMI2) (The National Archives 1999). PMI2 reflected the prevalent notion that students were an asset and in most cases not long-term immigrants as most, especially, non-EU students returned to their country of origin. In years to come, Conservative and coalition governments would struggle with this idea.

PMI2 was not only about international recruitment targets, although that was a significant part of it with a target of 100,000 new students 70,000 of them in higher education (The National Archives 1999).

The universities and British Council had done a good job with Broadening Our Horizons. And from this, PMI2 showed a better understanding of the complexities of working overseas and the notion of a gap between perceived as opposed to actual quality.

Increased international recruitment remained the priority, but there was now talk of 'growth of UK international education delivered not only in the UK but also overseas' (The National Archives 1999). This is in response to the increase in transnational education (TNE) activities being carried out by UK universities by 2006, most of which were being carried out with partners overseas.

The main thrust of PMI2 was still sell sell sell, with the Education@UK brand and marketing activities led by the British Council. But these were now not tasked with selling just UK-based programmes but also selling all UK higher education international activities. PMI2 objectives were to 'increase the number of international students undertaking UK education', whether at home or overseas.

DIVERSIFICATION OF MARKETS

There was recognition that there was a dependence on student numbers from a small number of countries which sent a large number of students to the UK. PMI2 had a stated target to double the numbers of countries that send more than 10,000 students to the UK.

This same desire was being articulated in many universities' international strategies. Most had some sort of statement that they wished to increase the spread of students in terms not only of country of origin but also in subjects studied. This was brought on by the huge numbers of mainly Chinese students studying business studies and there was every indication that the massive growth in Chinese students was set to continue.

But for most post-1992 universities, finding a market to replace existing successful ones was wishful thinking. Although they were working in an increasing global market, they were in competition not only with better placed UK universities but also with Australians, Americans with increasing activity from Malaysia and Europe.

The reality was that in post-1992 universities the total number of students was the ultimate target that the success of any strategy was measured against. After all, predicted numbers were translated into expected income and spend for the year ahead. Universities' targets were based on data from Vision 2020, which predicted significant growth year-on-year. And the majority of that growth was predicted to be in the same countries that were already sending the most students and in the same subject areas.

The base scenario of Vision 2020 predicted numbers from China rising from 26,800 in 2005 to 130,900 by 2020. Although there were some changes in the ordinal rank of non-EU markets, the top five was predicted to remain much the same. There was no indication that there was a major new market awaiting to emerge.

So individual universities' international recruitment teams still prioritised the existing major markets and the PMI2 also set these as some of their 24 non-EU priority markets. So it is no surprise that diversification targets were not achieved either by PMI2 or by individual post-1992 universities.

After all, it would have been a very unusual post-1992 university business school that sets limits on, say, the number of Chinese students it accepted, in an environment where they were in competition to have the largest international student population possible.

Russell Group Universities and those well placed in the league tables could make decisions on numbers from different countries as they rejected large numbers of applicants. Post-1992 universities seldom rejected any applicant who had the correct entry requirements unless it was for lab- or studio-based programmes which did not have enough specialist space or equipment to take more students. In mass education programmes, any new international student was considered to be of marginal cost as long as there was a lecture theatre big enough to squeeze them into. This meant that their fees could be considered as nearly 100 per cent profit – all of it spending money.

PMI2 funded two areas – student experience and employability to help address the differences between what the students had been promised and the reality that was highlighted in Broadening Our Horizons.

Bizarrely, the funding for employability was used to improve international students' employability in the UK rather than when they returned home.

By the end of PMI2, the UK Council for International Student Affairs (UKCISA) published a paper where they reviewed 'PMI Student Experience

Achievements 2006–2011' (UKCISA 2012) and they could proudly state that satisfaction with employability – whatever that is – had risen from 71 per cent to 78 per cent!

Integration with UK students was a major issue, especially when large numbers of students came from a single country, which is curious, because the whole philosophy of the 'student experience' strand of PMI2 revolved around treating the international student differently than their home counterparts.

At this point, only international students were contributing large amounts of their own money to universities and were being considered customers unlike home students. This would change in years to come with the introduction of full fees for home students.

DAMP SQUIB INTERNATIONAL PLANS 2013 AND 2018

With the Home Office in the driving seat, in July 2013, David Willets, the minister for Universities and Science, brought out a new strategy 'International Education Global Growth and Prosperity'. In effect, it positioned education among other business exports. Eight countries were targeted, including China, India, Saudi Arabia and one region (the Gulf).There was talk in the international strategy of a coordinated response to challenges', work with alumni when the students return home and a stronger focus on educational technology and TNE. But as always, it was all about the brand –linking education to the 'Great Britain Campaign'. A champion for UK education was announced, who would chair a new body called International Education Council and who would help ensure 'effective communication and engagement with all parts of the sector' even though most parts of the sector were in competition. The main barrier to students coming to the UK – visas and lack of job opportunities – were dismissed by claiming that it was just a matter of making sure we communicated that there was no 'cap on international student visas' and that there were still job opportunities for graduates to remain in the country (Willets 2013).

Basically, the strategy was a weak attempt to claim that the government wanted to support the increase of international student numbers. A table taken from HESA and the Department of Business Innovation and Skills showed three estimates of increase in numbers – a high 6.7 per cent per year, central 3.7 per cent per year and low 0.7 per cent increase per year until 2020. The aim of the strategy was to support the growth, at least the central growth estimate, and have 15–20 per cent growth over five years. This was not achieved, with student numbers only increasing from 435,000 in 2011/12 to 441,000 in 2016.

In March 2019, a further international strategy was published. As Nic Hillman in University World News pointed out, since the previous strategy in 2013, 'We have had five ministers for universities, four secretaries of state for education, three types of government (a coalition, a majority administration and a minority administration), two elections and one referendum' (Hillman 2019). Despite all this, the new strategy was a damp squib. Just more of the same as in 2013 – a champion for international education was to be appointed, an increase in the number of international students on-campus to 600,000 by 2030 this time, but no real change in what the government would do to actually help this happen. The same words about the UK being welcoming and there being no limit on student visas – but of course student numbers were still in net migration – the difference between the number of immigrants entering the country minus those leaving. The biggest item for international recruiters was a watered-down version of post-study work as the action point states: 'Government will strengthen the UK's visa offer for international higher education students by increasing the post-study leave period and making it easier for students to move into skilled work after graduation' (Dept. of Education 2019). But, of course, the detail would be up to the Home Office.

There was a tacit acknowledgement that increasing on-campus student numbers would remain challenging in the fact that the three action points that relate to assistance that the government would give to higher education were all in the areas of TNE. The first action point is particularly typical: 'The Department for Education and Department for International Trade will work with the higher education sector and the British Council to identify more accurately the overall value of TNE to the UK economy' (Dept. of Education 2019).

No doubt, this is to be followed by a paper that gives a 'more accurate', that is, a much larger guestimate of the contribution to the economy of TNE.

Currently, the guestimate is that TNE contributed in £1.9 billion towards the £14 billion that higher education exports were claimed to contribute to the UK economy in 2016 (British Council 2016).

However, whether this is less than reality or not, it shows on-campus student recruitment is far more profitable; in 2016 it was estimated that there were 466,000 on-campus international students and 700,000 TNE students. Given the higher risk involved in TNE and the relatively larger potential profit from on-campus students, it is no wonder that few of the top universities have mass TNE programmes with private for-profit organisations.

Within weeks of Boris Johnson becoming prime minister, he announced that students would be taken out of the net migration figures. This heralded a complete U-turn in Conservative thinking on international students. It is too early to see if this more welcoming regime will be able to compensate for the numbers of EU students that UK universities may lose.

CHAPTER 6

FRESH TALENT INITIATIVE: THE SCOTTISH GOVERNMENT PULLS A FAST ONE

FRESH TALENT INITIATIVE

Around the time of PMI2 wasn't just the UK government in Westminster that was doing everything to help universities expand overseas. The Devolved Parliament in Scotland was keen too. Scottish universities had long felt that they were at an unfair disadvantage in recruiting international students. Although their four-year undergraduate degree was in keeping with the majority of the world, it was not the norm throughout the rest of the UK.

For international students starting in year one, to get a degree from a Scottish university cost one year's more fees and living expenses than students studying a degree that was claimed to be of the same standard in England. And entry requirements were not so much different.

SCOTTISH PARLIAMENT GIVING SCOTTISH UNIVERSITIES AN ADVANTAGE

When the Scottish Parliament was set up, foreign affairs and immigration were maters that were reserved for Westminster. However, the Scottish Parliament under it's third First Minister Jack McConnell increasingly impinged in international affairs and even in immigration matters.

They set up the Scottish government's Scottish affairs offices in embassies throughout the world, which caused friction between Scottish government representatives and the UK government ones. At one point, the British Embassy in Beijing refused to allow the Scottish government's office to be located in their premises.

But for the Labour government in Westminster, by far the most irritating encroachment into reserved matters by the Scottish government was when the Labour leader of the government in Scotland brought in new immigration regulations –the Fresh Talent Initiative.

The Fresh Talent Initiative was designed to be a way of levelling the playing field for Scottish universities. Hiding under the pretence that there was a serious worry in Scotland of a decreasing population – despite the fact that another eight Eastern European countries had just joined the EU and their 74 million population now had the right to work and study in Scotland – Jack McConnell, in 2004, proposed his so-called the Fresh Talent Initiative. The main feature was a commitment to allow non-EU students who graduated from a Scottish university the right to work for two years after graduation.

In the foreword to the proposal 'Attracting Fresh Talent to Meet the Challenge of Growth' otherwise known as the Fresh Talent Initiative McConnell says: 'The most important thing that any government can do for its people is to act for the long term benefit of all, not to secure short term gain for a few.' And claims that, 'The single biggest challenge facing Scotland as we move further into the 21st century is our falling population' (McConnell 2004, 1).

This was a patent untruth and McConnell must have known it. Although there was a potential small dip in population predicted, it ignored the potential immigration from the A8 new EU countries.

With the A8 joining the EU, the Scottish-Polish immigrant community jumped from 2,052 to 55,000 in six years and continued to rise up to 76,000 (7.4 per cent of the population) by 2016. Most immigrants from the EU were young and there was a corresponding growth in birth rate. By 2011 the official statistics were predicting that Scotland's population would rise by 10 per cent by 2035. So much for the big challenge of a decreasing population.

And as for the Fresh Talent Initiative being about long-term benefit as McConnell claimed, the scheme had little to do with attracting long-term workers and talent to Scotland and all to do with attracting students who would stay long enough to pay for their education and then return home. In the foreword, McConnell states:

I believe migration into Scotland can play an important role in helping our economic future.

Not at the expense of older people, or those currently in the labour market. Nor somehow disregarding the talent we already have. In addition to our own talent though, we should look to fresh talent. (McConnell 2004)

The 6 per cent of the population that was at the time unemployed and the tens of thousands of women with skills and experience who couldn't work because of prohibitively high child care costs may have felt that their talents weren't quite fresh enough.

McConnell (2004) wrote, 'We have reached an agreement with the Home Office which will allow overseas graduates from Scottish universities, who express the intention of living and working in Scotland, to stay on for two years beyond the current October date, to seek employment'.

The initiative claimed that it was addressing the consequences of a declining and aging population, enhancing migration opportunities into Scotland, meeting labour shortages and increasing cultural diversity. No mention of what it actually was – a huge marketing ploy for Scottish universities to give them an edge over the rest of the UK.

Fresh Talent wasn't really about some shortage in skill; McConnell didn't really want to look for fresh talent. Students who had just graduated with a degree could hardly be classified as highly skilled workers. The reality was that the initiative did not require that the jobs were of graduate calibre but would allow any graduate a visa for any job no matter how menial and how little talent, fresh or otherwise, was required.

This was all about increasing Scotland's attractiveness to overseas students in comparison to the rest of the UK. It was a cunning move to stay part of Education@UK – world-class traditional quality but then add a bonus. Scotland as the most welcoming part of the UK. And boy did it work.

But when it was announced, the agreement with the Home Office was not quite as fixed as McConnell was letting on. Announcements about the Fresh Talent Initiative had been made long prior to any agreement to allow a differential visa regime between Scotland and the rest of the UK. All Scottish universities were aware that the Scottish government had said that they could and would deliver on it. This left the Home Secretary David Blunkett with a dilemma; only he could decide whether to allow it or not. The question was, was he going to embarrass a Labour first minister or not? Not only that, how could he possibly allow different immigration rules north and south of the border? There were no passport controls between Scotland and England so what would stop students with the right to remain just driving across the border to work? And how would he square this with the English universities?

He allowed the Fresh Talent Initiative to be put in place, but insisted that it was a pilot scheme only, which would be closely monitored as part of a managed immigration policy. McConnell was busy claiming that his was a uniquely

Scottish initiative that heralded a change to how devolved nations could be treated. The BBC news reported that McConnell told Parliament, 'This is an immensely important signal. It is the first time there has been this kind of flexibility within the UK immigration system' (BBC News 2004).

And at the same time Blunkett was stating that the Fresh Talent Initiative was a pilot scheme for the whole of UK.

But in McConnell's rhetoric it wasn't a pilot scheme, as only Scotland was eligible as the only country in the UK with a potential decrease in population. This was strongly denied by Westminster (Peterkin 2004).

Universities throughout the UK were well aware of the trick the Scottish universities had played and looked on with a mixture of admiration and jealousy. They realised that Scottish institutions had been given a huge advantage in luring foreign students by offering them residency after graduation.

Post-1992 universities were particularly active in marketing the opportunities that having two years' post-study work offered. There was no stipulation that the jobs that these so-called talented individuals would take had to be of graduate level.

In price-sensitive countries, particularly India, the opportunity to stay and work in Scotland was marketed as a way of paying back fees.

A number of clever schemes were developed. One Indian hospitality college developed relationships with a number of post-1992 Scottish universities, taking advantage of the potential to work in any level of job for two years after graduation.

Students who had completed a two-year diploma in the college in India, much of it of a practical nature, were accepted into third year of the Scottish universities' hospitality degrees. They then left after one year with an ordinary degree and entered the workforce for two years.

The college in India even had an office in Scotland, which helped find employment for these graduates who had spent two years in the college in Kolkata and Delhi, learning how to cook authentic curries and work in the hospitality trade. There were plenty of jobs in the hospitality sector, which would be considered as badly paying by indigenous graduates but they were hoovered up by these young people who had spent their extended families' savings to allow them the opportunity.

For the years that the visas allowed students to work, this group of colleges in India were sending several hundred students a year to Scotland. When they were recruited in India, they were guaranteed a job in the UK by the college, the fees were heavily discounted as the college was supplying large numbers to the universities. It was a win-win situation – better level of cooking in one's favourite Indian restaurant and students who returned home with a UK degree, work experience and even some money.

With the ingenuity of post-1992 universities and private partners, agents, colleges and so on throughout the world, Fresh Talent was a huge success. We know that because when the automatic right for graduates to work was stopped, post-1992 universities were hit particularly hard. The four post-1992 universities that recruited the most Indian students lost 80 per cent of their intake (HESA n.d.).

REST OF THE UK WANTING THEIR SHARE OF THE PIE

But the rest of the UK was not fooled by the idea that Fresh Talent was about a declining population. An article in the *Times* by John Lessware on 22 October 2005, entitled 'Foreign Students Flock to Scotland', highlighted the concerns: 'Vice-chancellors at institutions south of the border have blamed the Scottish executive's Fresh Talent Initiative for a slump in applications from foreigners while those in Scotland have risen by more than 20 per cent' (Lessware 2005).

Applications from India, previously weighted 80/20 in favour of English universities, are now 70/30 in favour of the Scottish ones. There has also been a large rise in the number of Chinese students applying to Scotland.

The vice chancellor of Liverpool University who was also president of Universities UK was quoted in the *Times* article as saying,

> 'There is no doubt that Fresh Talent has made Scotland more attractive than England. That is the key reason there has been such a big shift away from the English universities.
>
> We are lobbying very hard and I have been talking to Tony McNulty to try and get the initiative extended to the whole of the UK. It's very important. It's long been known that the ability to get a job and stay on for a bit is a very big factor in people's choices.
>
> We have been speaking to our agents overseas and they have said that being able to work is one of the determining factors as to where people go to study.

It is telling that the largest increases of applications noted in the *Sunday Times* were from post-1992 universities. The fact that they attracted more students who wished to take work in the UK for two years after graduation is most probably an indication that these students were poorer.

At a 28 June 2005, meeting of the Joint Education Taskforce, a pan-UK body created by the Home Office, civil servants heard university representatives question the right of the Scottish Executive to operate a separate regime on a reserved issue such as immigration.

Grievances were aired about Fresh Talent only applying to Scotland, as university groups in England and Wales argued it should apply across the UK.

A spokeswoman for universities UK admitted there was frustration in England regarding Fresh Talent.

'It is incredibly positive from a Scottish perspective. But we would like some of it too,' she said. 'Any bemusement comes from the fact that the visa system is UK-wide. Students who come to Scotland on Fresh Talent might not stay there. There's nothing to stop them leaving'. (workpermit.com 2005)

To try to calm down the irate universities from the rest of the UK, the government introduced the Post-Study Work Visa (PSW) for the rest of the UK. However, this was initially limited to allow STEM graduates to remain in the UK for one year's work experience. This was nowhere as flexible as the Fresh Talent scheme, which allowed any graduate two years visa. So, after more lobbying, PSW gradually became more open and more generous (Migration Watch UK 2012). The final version, brought in on May 2008 as part of the new points-based immigration system called Tier 1 Post-Study Work, allowed all graduates of any discipline and any degree class to remain in the UK for up to two years in order to search for work with no restrictions on their skill levels, thus ending the edge that the Scottish government had given Scottish universities.

The rest of the UK followed the Scottish model. Universities at the bottom of league tables sold PSW as a way for students who couldn't actually afford a UK education to pay for one afterwards with hard labour. To get a visa required evidence of sufficient funds but there are well-known ways around this, even companies set up just for this purpose.

So poor students came to the UK with the express goal to work as many hours as they could and spend as little in the two years allocated.

The majority of students who took advantage of the opportunity did not have graduate-level jobs.

When the United Kingdom Border Agency (UKBA) was asked to look at PSW in 2010, they found that less than 10 per cent of Tier 1 visas that came in through the PSW route could be confirmed to have what would be considered skilled work.

After PSW was revoked, the numbers of Indian students studying in the UK halved. There were also downturns in other price-sensitive countries. The drop in Indian numbers was not even throughout the sector, with the brunt being felt by post-1992 institutions (HESA 2013).

CHAPTER 7

CHANGES IN ATTITUDES TOWARDS IMMIGRATION – BOGUS COLLEGES AND DODGY DIPLOMAS

Around the time of the Fresh Talent Initiative from 2005 to 2008, there was increasing anti-immigration rhetoric in the UK press. Nigel Farage was voted leader of UKIP. Stories of MPs of all parties with their snouts in the trough of parliamentary expenses abounded with a subsequent distrust of mainstream politicians. UKIPs anti-immigration and anti-EU stance began to gain traction with mainstream voters. The spectre of the shires of England being overrun by Romanians and Bulgarians when the A2 states acceded to the EU was played out in the press and by the UKIP and the right of centre Conservatives. It didn't matter that the UK government had restricted the A2's right to enter the country. In 2007 the Labour prime minister Gordon Brown negotiated the Lisbon Treaty. The treaty greatly altered the way members govern themselves. It created an EU president and a vastly more powerful foreign policy chief for the union's 27 nations. According to many Conservatives, this was the biggest threat to national sovereignty in Europe since the Second World War.

Those opposing the treaty, claimed that it was just a reworking of the European Constitution that the French and Netherlands had rejected in a referendum. According to them, the Lisbon Treaty showed how the unelected Brussels bureaucrats rode roughshod over the wills of the people. Like the rejected European Constitution, the Lisbon Treaty was considered a blueprint for a European super state dreamt up by unelected bureaucrats in Brussels. Some demanded a referendum on the treaty, but although the Irish had two referendums as the first one rejected the treaty, Brown did not allow one.

UKIP and others claimed that this was an example of how democracy was too dangerous a concept for the architects of the grand vision of an EU superpower. It didn't help that Brown was so lukewarm about the treaty that he didn't attend the signing ceremony. The signing of the Lisbon Treaty was a big step towards Brexit and the beginning of a hardening view of immigration that would affect the overseas student market.

Luckily for universities, UKIP and the right did not find out that the easiest way to get in the country illegally was through the student visa system.

The Home Office were well aware that they had not put immigration processes in place fit for purpose with dealing with the massive increase in international student numbers. The old cosy system, where universities were attracting the best of the best with scholarships or very rich international students, had at its heart an element of trust that was ripe for exploitation by people who were not people like us.

Before 2008, when a points-based system was phased in, the cheapest, safest and easiest way for an illegal immigrant to enter the country was by applying to study in the UK and enter with bona fide visas. Most were through entities set up just for this purpose. But it was also easy for unscrupulous people to use universities.

Universities only had a duty to check that the student was qualified to enter their programme and that duty was only internal to the university.

To get into the country 'legally' through this route required a filled-in application form, complete with photocopies of the applicant's qualifications – the originals had to be handed over when matriculating. These were sent or faxed to the university, or in some case an agent. Based on this flimsy evidence, the applicant would be given an offer letter, which would be used to apply for a visa. In many cases, particularly for post-1992 universities, agents in country were given the authority to make offers on behalf of the university and could print their own offer letters. Or visiting staff from the university would hand out offer letters after interviewing students. Only the few top universities required a deposit before they gave an offer letter. The rest were too worried about scaring off a potential student.

The visa application stage was a bit more difficult as one had to show that there was enough money in a bank account to stay in the UK and sometimes there was an interview. But for enough money this could be arranged. And if it didn't work, you hadn't risked your life or even left your country of origin.

If it did work and you were granted a visa, you just flew to the UK, entered legally and disappeared and no one was the wiser. And it had cost only the price of a visa and flight.

The universities or colleges in the UK were not informed by the Home Office of any visas that had been awarded on the bases of their offer letter.

So the universities were aware of how many offers they had made and had to wait with bated breath to see how many students actually turned up.

If someone who had been made an offer did not turn up, the university did not inform the Home Office of this. After all they didn't know whether the applicant had decided they couldn't afford it, taken another offer, been refused a visa or one of many reasons that they might not arrive.

And anyway they wouldn't be able to tell the Home Office who hadn't turned up because of data protection regulations!

So the Home Office knew how many visas they had issued, and the universities knew how many students they had made offers to and how many didn't turn up, but kept that information to themselves. There were no checks made by the Home Office to see how many students who entered the country with a visa based on an offer letter from a university actually went on to study at that university.

It didn't take long for unscrupulous individuals and organisations to take advantage of this lack of coherence in the student visa system.

To this day there is no way of knowing how many illegal immigrants used this method of getting into the country. However, we do know that some universities had eye-watering attrition rates. The British Universities International Liaison Group (BUILA), which hosted a forum to discuss application and recruitment issues, found that for planning purposes most post-1992 universities worked on a ration of 15 offer letters which had been accepted for every 'bum on seat' for most countries. But some countries were so bad that when estimating numbers of students that you expected based on offer letters, you had to discount them completely. It was not unusual to have 50 offers to Nigerian applicants, all of which had been accepted by the students, resulting in only one student appearing – and who knows how many visas were issued. It wasn't just post-1992 universities that had this problem. But as organisations that had to actively recruit, they were more likely to offer a place and less likely to need a deposit than many attractive pre-1992 universities who had the good luck to have more applicants than places.

As the recruitment process became increasingly target-based, there were more and more offers made. Some universities had bonus schemes based solely on the number of offers made. As one Dean of International put it, 'if you throw enough mud at the wall some of it will stick'.

In some countries applying to a UK university with false documentation became so commonplace that examples of forgeries were circulated between universities so they could identify bogus applicants. But that was so the universities didn't waste time or effort in processing those applications rather than to highlight them to the Home Office. There was a fear of getting the Home Office involved because the decision-making process for granting visas was seen as very subjective at the time and no one wanted to get a reputation of being a destination for dodgy applications.

In one recruitment fair in Lahore, staff returned from an unusually alcohol-free lunch to find that their printed letterhead paper, which they used to make on-the-spot offers, had disappeared.

In a few months border agents were coping with large numbers of individuals who could not speak any English and had appeared in an airport hundreds of miles from the university they were meant to be studying at.

Eventually a so-called agent in Lahore was identified as being the source of these bogus students. She had taken the letter heads and was selling offer letters to anyone with the money to pay for them. She was even advertising in the newspaper. Even though this was discovered, nothing could be done by the Home Office, apart from ensuring the visa office in Pakistan was aware of it. Those universities that had lost their letterheads no longer got any students from Pakistan as not even the real students were given visas.

But the focus of attention was not on universities but on the thousands of completely bogus English language colleges that were opened in the UK to take advantage of the ease of getting student visas. Where universities could be considered innocent bystanders to visa abuse, these colleges were where visa abuse was being carried out deliberately and on an industrial scale.

In the UK until 2004, unlike publically funded education providers, private education providers were not regulated by the state. This allowed for the easy formation of an English language school or even college.

Private colleges only had to register as a business; any other regulation of them was on a voluntary basis. Thousands of colleges sprung up just to sell visas.

Some didn't even have premises but were able to sell offer letters to people who wanted to enter the country illegally. They were in fact people traffickers, and a back door into the country or a way of extending illegal immigrants' stay. For £1,000 you could get an offer letter and for a further £2,500, a bogus evidence of attendance and a diploma or even degree (Ford 2004). It was also possible to pay these colleges to give documentation to show you had sufficient money in the bank to pay fees and living expenses. According to Labour's Immigration Minister Phil Woolas, 'Abuse of the student visa has been the biggest abuse of the system, the major loophole in Britain's border controls' (House of Commons Home Affairs Commitee 2009).

THE FAILURE OF VISA CHANGES TO STOP BOGUS COLLEGES

It was well known that bogus colleges were operating visa scams ; in an article in the *Times* by Richard Ford on 23 July 2004, it was said that 'Officials believe that more than two thirds of 672 colleges checked in London are operating as front organisations, allowing migrants to evade immigration control' (Ford 2004). As early as 2005, Chris Mullins, member of parliament, had noted in his diaries that the 'scale of the fraud is awesome: "students" applying for courses that don't exist in colleges that don't exist, supported by documents that are forged. What are we going to do?' (Mullins 2009).

With the discussions around PMI2, from 2004 the Home Office was consulted in areas that affected migration policy. The Home Office recommended that the issue of bogus colleges needed to be dealt with immediately and a new points-based system for immigration should be developed.

But with PMI2 about to begin, Universities UK, the body which represents the principals and vice chancellors of UK universities, lobbied to make sure that any methods to control bogus colleges would not interfere with their recruitment efforts, and their pressure ensured the continued existence of these colleges for many more years.

On 18 June 2004, Charles Clarke, the then secretary of state for the department for education and skills, made it clear that although the issue of bogus colleges would be addressed, the priority should be to ensure that the money from international students continued to flow into the country. To him and his government, universities' income from international students was more important than making sure that there was no abuse of the visa system. In a speech to the house entitled, 'Register of Learning Providers', Clarke quoted Vision 2020: 'Student mobility is a welcome feature of 21st century globalisation and we benefit from it. The recent British Council report showed that students from overseas currently contribute £3 billion a year to the UK economy' (Clarke 2014).

He then outlined a few measures to ensure that English language providers were not bogus, saying that they were 'encouraging English language schools to seek accreditation with existing bodies such as the British Council or the Association of British Language Schools'.

In addition, he said that they were looking at

measures to ensure that students attending other private education providers are able to receive genuine opportunities. Partly for this purpose, the Department for Education and Skills has been developing plans for a Register of Educational Providers and I can now announce that this will be in place by the end of the year. We will then make the register available to the Home Office to support them in making their decisions on granting leave to study. They propose only to issue leave to study to students attending providers on the register. (Clarke 2014)

One would think that this would solve the problem. But far from stopping bogus colleges it proved to be a license to print money.

The register of education providers (REP) did the opposite of what it intended, as it actually validated bogus colleges. From 2005, when the REP was instigated to 2009, when it was eventually replaced, over 4,000 colleges were registered. And when you were on the REP, you were genuine, a real education provider as attested to by none other than the UK government.

The House of Commons Home Affairs Committee Bogus Colleges Report 2009 (House of Commons Home Affairs Commitee 2009) shows that between the introduction of the REP in January 2005 and the report in 2009, the system was being widely abused. The report details that

> Private institutions without accreditation were also able to get on the REP by providing evidence of their registration as a legal business with Companies House; details of their staff and staff qualifications; floor plans to show classrooms and other facilities; and a copy of their prospectus to give an indication of the teaching they provided. (House of Commons Home Affairs Commitee 2009)

It didn't require an inspection, and inspections were only 'reactive, intelligence-led visits to suspect colleges on the REP'. It didn't take a criminal mastermind to see that the REP was in fact a way of gaining easy legitimacy.

It only cost £12 to register a company with Companies House and then a few days' work to acquire floor plans of an office, which you either didn't own or you rented for a few months, write a prospectus and write a list of staff and their qualifications. The odds of being physically checked were low and even then, advanced notice was given of any visits and even some of the accrediting companies were suspect (House of Commons Home Affairs Commitee 2009). In the *Times* it was reported that a former head of international operations, who had been sacked from a new university for unspecified misdemeanours, had set up a private company to conduct assessments of colleges that wished to be included in the register. The company had been accredited to carry out assessments and was based in 'a semi-detached house in a village near Middleburgh'. Although the reasons for dismissal were not disclosed, it was said that the university had written to the Home Office to question the role it would have in accrediting colleges. Later, Universities UK wrote to Liam Byrne, the immigration minister to 'express concern about the decision' to approve the company as one of the accreditation bodies. However, the Home Office claimed it was up to Ofsted to decide on accreditation and Ofsted said that they 'were satisfied that it was operating in a satisfactory manner' (Norfolk 2009).

As the Home Affairs report into bogus colleges stated in bold no less, **'Insufficient quality assurance procedures on the part of the Department for Innovations, Universities and Skills for private educational establishments on the Register of Education Providers, which facilitated the issuing of student visas between 2005 and 2009, allowed bogus colleges to bring foreign nationals into the UK on fraudulent student visas'** (House of Commons Home Affairs Commitee 2009). When asked by the Home Affairs Committee as to how many illegal immigrants may have come through the student visa route, the chief executive of English UK, the body that represented English language colleges, Tony Mullins said, 'It could be tens of thousands quite easily', and as the representative of English language colleges, it was in his interest to downplay the reality!

POINTS-BASED SYSTEM

During the time the Home Affairs Committee Report into Bogus Colleges was written, the Labour government had phased in a new points-based system which, among other things, closed the feedback loop between education providers and the Home Office. Under the new points-based system, all work permits and entry schemes, including the Fresh Talent Scheme Initiative were replaced with tiers. Points were allocated for qualifications, expected earnings, sponsorship, English language skill and available maintenance.

Tier 4 was for student visas. Education providers had to apply to be sponsors. Under the points-based system, an employer or education provider who wanted to recruit international students needed to have a license. When licensed, they were added to the register of sponsors. The system was managed by UK Border Agency the predecessor of UK Visas and Immigration. On 31 March 2009, the register of sponsors replaced the REP. This allowed the Home Office to close the loop and made sponsors responsible for checking and reporting on any visa transgressions of students that they sponsored.

Tier 4 sponsors had to report to the Home Office if the student failed to enrol on his/her course within the enrolment period; if the student missed 10 expected contacts without their Tier 4 sponsor's permission; if the Tier 4 sponsor stopped being the student's immigration sponsor for any other reason, for example, if the student moved into an immigration category that did not need a Tier 4 sponsor; if there were any significant changes in the student's circumstances; or if it became apparent that the student was breaking the conditions of their permission to stay.

All universities were given what was called Highly Trusted Status, which meant they did not have to be accredited at the start. But this could be revoked for a number of reasons including sponsoring too many students who were refused visas or who did not attend the university after being issued with a visa.

This in effect put paid to the previous behaviour of making large volumes of offers and expecting a large attrition rate. The sponsor was made responsible for ensuring that the applicant was bone fide – they had to check bank accounts as well as ensure that qualifications were valid. Most began to ask for a deposit of several thousand pounds before agreeing to sponsor students, which was unheard of in the post-1992 sector before sponsorship. Agents were no longer allowed to issue offer letters and on-the-spot offers were rare.

As you can imagine, universities were less than happy with this new responsibility and argued to no avail through Universities UK that they should be treated as a special case.

Bogus colleges found it harder to operate, but not impossible.

The Home Affairs Report noted that when the REP was replaced with the more rigorously policed list of approved sponsors in 2009, more than half the colleges on the REP (nearly 2,200 colleges) did not register under the more stringent regulations (House of Commons Home Affairs Commitee 2009). Commenting on these figures, the minister of state for borders and immigration said:

> One could draw the conclusion […] that the difference is dodgy. (House of Commons Home Affairs Commitee 2009)

One might wonder why it took until 2009 for the introduction of a system to ensure that those with visas to study were in fact studying. After all there was a war on terrorism going on and immigration was becoming a major issue with the electorate.

But with PMI and PMI2 having the prime minister's stamp of approval, universities had powerful friends in the government. Any new regulations that might inconvenience universities' international recruitment or make the UK seem less welcoming were denounced as unfair by Universities UK. The international recruitment juggernaut was not going to be derailed by a few – well a few thousand – bogus colleges. There was no wish in the government to hamper PMI2 or indeed to stand up to Universities UK, so nothing was done – they just hoped no one would notice, particularly Nigel Farage.

But unfortunately for them, by 2009 after repeated headlines in the press about bogus student visas, there was an article in the *Times* that attracted more serious attention. And it was as a direct result of that *Times* article that the inquiry which formed the report of the Home Affairs Committee Report on Bogus Colleges was carried out (House of Commons Home Affairs Commitee 2009).

The *Times* put the cat among the pigeons in May 2009 with its headline 'Sham Colleges Open Doors to Pakistani Terror Suspects' (Norfolk 2009), which really got the attention of the politicians, and thus meant they could not ignore the phenomenon. The article detailed the arrest of a businessman for setting up a bogus college. This college had been on the REP since 2007 when it had been accredited by the very body that the Home Office and the minister for immigration had been warned about by Universities UK. That didn't stop the same company being allowed to help accredit sponsors on the new scheme.

One telling detail in the article was that 'Two Liverpool universities have admitted they gave places to four "graduates" from one of the bogus colleges.' These students had gone from being illegal immigrants with visas supplied by bogus colleges to individuals on genuine student visas. But the main issue was not with post-1992 universities or pre-1992 universities taking students from dodgy colleges. It was that the principals and vice chancellors exerted pressure through Universities UK, which ensured that sensible measures that would curb visa abuses took a very long time to be implemented.

CHANGE IN ATTITUDES TO IMMIGRATION

In the 2010 general election, immigration became a battleground. The *Daily Mail* claimed that 98.7 per cent of all jobs created from 1997 had been taken by immigrants (Chapman 2010).The highly selective figures were gleaned from the Office for National Statistics and were originally highlighted on the Spectator's Coffee House blog.

The then prime minister, Gordon Brown, claimed that net migration was going down, only to have to back down and admit to a misuse of immigration statistics after a Tory complaint was upheld by the head of UK Statistics Authority.

Brown then claimed that his new points-based visa system would address the issues with non-skilled workers entering the country, but could not shake off the accusation that Labour had opened the doors to all. Surprisingly, the issue of dodgy students did not feature much in the debate.

No one actually looked closely at how for 20 years up to the introduction of sponsorship, aggressively recruiting universities had been allowing students in the country because they had a culture of accepting every student that looked like they might have the entry qualifications and just hoping they turned up.

To appease a significant section of his party and the growing mood of the electorate in the run-up to the election in May 2010, David Cameron signed a document in front of the cameras, which was titled, 'A Contract between the Conservative Party and You.' In it he made five pledges that he would guarantee to honour if he was elected. Number five was to 'Control immigration, reducing it to the levels of the 1990s – meaning tens of thousands a year instead of the hundreds of thousands a year under Labour' (Cameron 2010).

This was going to come back and haunt him years later, as he and his Home Secretary Theresa May failed to meet the targets he set. But it helped the Tories oust Labour and form a coalition government with the Liberal Democrats.

STUDENTS AS PART OF NET MIGRATION

The game was up. The light-touch immigration policy for students that had overseen an increase in international students in the UK to over 300,000 and created the easiest way to get into the country illegally was replaced.

With the incoming coalition government, the civil servants in the Home Office had found an ally in the fight against the abuses of the student visa system. Labour's education, education, education was replaced with immigration, immigration, immigration. Previously, education reigned supreme, and getting as many fee-paying students to the UK overrode any fears from the Home Office about systematic student visa abuses. In 2010 the boot was placed firmly on the other foot.

The main driver for government initiatives to increase international student numbers had been to make up for a gap in funding. However, the cap on home fees was being raised to £9,000, which would mean that the UK system – outwith Scotland – would become one of the best funded in the world. The government may have reasoned that given the cost of recruiting overseas, including agents' fees and discounts at £9,000, a home student would become more financially attractive than an international one. So they could make it more difficult for universities to recruit internationally with few consequences – for top universities at least – who would have the pick of fee-paying home students to fill their places and coffers.

There were going to be changes, and the university sector was worried. In its formal response to a consultation on changes to the immigration system that were being proposed, Universities UK was adamant:

> Universities UK strongly opposes the majority of the proposals outlined in the consultation. This position arises from our view that the proposals would have a substantial negative impact on individual universities, the wider economy and the global reputation of the UK as a destination that welcomes international students and recognises the significant contribution that they make. (Universities UK 2011, 5)

Despite these comments and intense lobbying from Universities UK, the Home Secretary Theresa May published a consultation document, 'Major Changes to The Student Visa System', where she said:

> The government has committed to reforming all routes of entry to the UK in order to bring immigration levels under control, international students not only make a vital contribution to the UK economy but they also help make our education system one of the best in the world.

> But it has become very apparent that the old student visa regime failed to control immigration and failed to protect legitimate students from poor quality colleges

> The student changes will work alongside the annual limit on economic migration, and reforms to family and settlement routes planned for later this year. (May 2011)

May was clear that she would deal with bogus colleges, many of which were still managing to operate under the new sponsorship scheme. In a speech in the house detailing her changes to the immigration policy, she seemed to calm the fears of universities by saying:

> But nearly half of all students coming here from abroad are actually coming to study a course below degree level and abuse is particularly common at these lower levels – a recent check of students studying at private institutions below degree level showed that a quarter could not be accounted for. (May 2011)

But what she never said outright was that she also had post-1992 universities in her sights as well.

On the college front, she was briefed that the changes that Brown's government had made to introduce the points-based system were not stringent enough. And that even though 2,200 bogus colleges which had formerly been on the REP had not registered to be visa sponsors, there were still bogus providers out there. One loophole that remained was that newly opened colleges were allowed to operate for at least six months before they were given an accreditation visit. There were still concerns about the credibility of some of the private companies that had been tasked with these accreditation visits and it often took much longer than six months before any visit was made. If a college was closed it could reopen under a new name the next day.

So it was no surprise that May introduced a more strict sponsorship scheme.

From April 2012 all institutions wanting to sponsor students will have to be classed as 'highly trusted sponsors' and become accredited by statutory education inspection bodies by the end of 2012.

The current system does not require this and allowed too many poor quality colleges into the system. (May 2011)

The Highly Trusted Sponsor (HTS) system was far more rigorous than the previous sponsorship. In the previous sponsorship system introduced by the outgoing Brown administration in 2010, all degree-awarding institutions needed to have HTS, but sub-degree level providers did not. From 2012, all institutions who wanted to recruit international students had to apply for HTS. As before, institutions were to be assessed on a points-based system, but there were far more inspections. After it was introduced, a further 900 colleges were closed. This meant that from when the old register of education providers was in place, when there were 4,000 colleges that could give official acceptance letters, 2,200 had not registered to be sponsors, and then when HTS came in, a further 900 were closed down. One could surmise, as a previous minster of state had, that this meant there had been 3,100 'dodgy' colleges!

Although the HTS was granted to all UK universities, it was made clear that this was a gift from the government which could be revoked at any time. With the insistence of including all students in net immigration statistics, it was becoming plain to post-1992 universities that they were now considered suspect or, even worse, the Home Secretary was going to stop them from recruiting international students.

The writing was on the wall if you knew where to look. As I wrote in an article in the THES in reaction to Cameron's stated aim to reduce immigration to the tens of thousands:

> Students contribute the largest figure to these statistics – even though several select committees have proposed that they are counted separately. The problem is that, overseas students leaving the country are counted out, but as the average undergraduate degree is three years long (four in Scotland), there will always be more in the country than leaving. Thus, even though evidence suggests that by far the majority will leave, overseas students are still the largest contributor to the net migration statistics. And so that is the place where cuts have to be made to make the unrealistic net migration targets the Tories are craving. (Brady 2013b)

In years to come, May would refuse to take students out of the net migration figures even though the Tories were not getting anywhere near the tens of thousands they promised. Given that net migration in 2010 was estimated to be around 255,000 by the Home Office and students contributed nearly 100,000 of this (IPPR 2012), it would have made the job of May's government easier just to deduct them from the figures. But May didn't believe that the UK should be taking in as many students and she definitely didn't think that post-1992 universities should be doing so. She stated in the introduction to her changes to the system that,

> The changes I am announcing today re-focus the student route as a temporary one, available to only the brightest and best. The new system is designed to ensure students come for a limited period, to study not work, and make a positive contribution while they are here. (May 2011)

This theme of only the brightest and best was continued by all senior Tories commenting on the new student visa system.

According to Damian Green, the immigration minister in 2010:

> Most people think foreign students come here to attend our top universities and of course these are the students we want to attract [...] It is beyond dispute that Britain's universities contain some of the best in the world and that they need to be competing for the world's best students. The immigration system should help them in this. But this does not mean that every student visa issued is necessarily benefiting Britain. (Green 2010)

During an immigration speech in 2010, Cameron continued the theme: 'Now, that means ensuring that those who do come here are the brightest and the best' (Cameroon 2010).

As 3 of the 17 out of 22 cabinet ministers who studied at Oxford or Cambridge, Cameron, May and Green's views of what constitutes 'brightest and best' was defined by their university experience, where the brightest and best from around the world are deliberately courted through schemes such as the Rhodes Scholarship for future world leaders. It was about soft power not funding.

It was plain that post-1992 universities with their flexible entry requirements, heavily discounted students with poor English who were working to pay off their fees were not the type of students they felt were the brightest and best. So they went about making it harder to recruit these students.

ENGLISH LANGUAGE LEVEL

Theresa May felt that many international students were gaining visas with a poor level of English language and she wanted to ensure that this would not continue. She stated:

> Those coming to study at degree level will have to speak a higher level of English than now. UK Border Agency staff will be able to refuse entry to students who cannot speak English without an interpreter and who therefore do not meet the required standards. (May 2012)

The minimum level was changed from B1 to B2 in the Common European Framework of Reference (CEFR). But on top of this, there were only certain Selected English Language Tests (SELTs) that universities were allowed to use.

Before then, it had been up to the university to decide which tests they considered to be secure. Some had developed their own tests and had sent staff out to administer these tests. In many cases the staff administering the test were not English language experts or even academics, but were members of the international recruitment team or even agents.

The new proposed regulations tried to put an end to universities' own testing. There were a small number of designated SELTs allowed and only these could be now used to measure B2 level not the universities' own tests or other tests such as the Chinese school English test, which individual universities had in the past decided were secure.

A list of countries that could be exempted from English language requirements was published by the Home Office.

This hurt some universities that individually had designated whole countries such as India and Nigeria where they claimed the language of instruction was predominantly English and so no IELTS was required.

The English language stipulations did not affect traditional universities as much, as English language requirements were higher.

Universities UK took umbrage at the idea that anyone outwith a university could make these types of decisions in the reply to the consultation question, which came out before May's report: 'Do you think all students using Tier 4 should have English at least B2 level?' Universities UK replied:

> This proposal has two dimensions: widening the scope of secure English language testing to include degree-level study, and raising the minimum level of study from B1 to B2. Universities UK does not support either of these proposals as autonomous higher education institutions have the right to – and are the most appropriate organisations to – determine their own admission requirements, including English language competence. As the Department for Business, Innovation and Skills (BIS) stated in 200917: '… the principle of university autonomy means that Government does not interfere with any university's admissions procedures.'
>
> Instead of applying such blanket restrictions UKBA should actually trust the academic judgements made by universities in relation to the recruitment and admission of students and not seek to impose arbitrary conditions in areas beyond their competence and beyond their immigration remit. (Universities UK 2011, 26)

This was a tacit admission that those universities that used their own English language tests were allowing students, who would not pass one of the newly designated SELTs, in.

They pulled the old 'we are autonomous' card and it worked. Universities were given permission to decide on which English language tests they accepted, or use their own method of assessing English language rather than only sticking to the recommended SELTs.

But it was understood that if the student was interviewed, either in-country or at the border, and they failed to convince the official interviewing them that they could speak passable English, certificate or not, they would be refused a visa or entry to the country. This would count against the university who had sponsored the student and they could potentially lose their licence. To this day there have been a few blips, but in general this threat has been severe enough to make sure universities are very careful about how they conduct their own tests, or they make sure that any students they pass have good interview training.

POST-STUDY WORK

The UKBA (2010) had done research into Tier 1 visa route and they found that 25 per cent were in skilled work. However, Tier 1 included skilled immigrants. In a table splitting Tier 1 visas into categories, of 253 Tier 1 Post-Study Work category visa holders, 153 were in unskilled work, 77 had an unclear work status and 23 were in skilled work, so around 10 per cent PSW visa holders were in skilled employment. So it was no surprise when May announced that the 'post-study work route, which allowed students two years to seek employment after their course ended will close'.

This hit certain markets worse than others. The Indian market was particularly badly hit. In the year that post-study work was stopped, numbers fell from over 39,000 to 22,000 with a continuous drop thereafter until 2016–17. Over five years the numbers of Indian students studying in the UK more than halved. But this was not evenly distributed throughout the sector; while Russell Group Universities saw a downturn of 25 per cent over that period, post-1992 universities saw a decrease of 70 per cent, with some post-1992 universities losing nearly 100 per cent of their Indian intake (HESA n.d.). This is a reflection of the fact that post-1992 universities had been more active in using post-study work as a sales technique in India.

Universities UK carped about the limited data to prove that the majority of post-study work visas were for unskilled work and the negative impression that removing this option gave overseas but to no avail.

There was an opportunity for students to stay in the country after graduation through Tier 2 but only if they had real demonstrable graduate-level jobs.

In 2011 when May introduced her new regulations, she claimed: 'My aim is not to stop genuine students coming here – it is to eliminate abuse within the system. Our stricter accreditation process will see only first class education providers given licences to sponsor students' (May 2011).

Those universities that did not think May would consider them as 'first class education providers' quaked in their campuses. After all, with HTS she had the tools to deal with them. Once you had been given HTS it could be taken off you.

As before, the university had to monitor attendance, keep copies of documents such as passports, ATAS (Academic Technology Approval Scheme) clearance, and up-to-date addresses, report non-enrolment and withdrawals. But there were to be compliance visits and no one was quite sure what level of non-compliance would lose a universities HTS.

There was talk about the level of visa refusals allowed being set at 2 per cent, which was frighteningly low. By 2015 HTS was no longer referred to and universities were just Tier 4 sponsors. Compliance was managed by UKVI United Kingdom Visas and Immigration), which was formed in 2013. By 2017, visa refusal rate was set at 10 per cent, enrolment rate of 90 per cent and a pass rate of 85 per cent.

From the start of the abolition of post-study work, there has been a constant demand to bring it back by Universities UK, the Scottish government and individual groups of universities. All quoted compelling evidence that those countries with more liberal post-study work regimes were attracting an increasing percentage of the world market.

But with the Conservative government's determination to have net migration in the tens of thousands and to keep students in the figures, the argument about how you could attract more students fell on deaf ears – until Boris Johnston bumbled into Number 10. Within a few weeks, he gave up the pledge on net migration, took students out of the net migration figures and reinstated in full the post-study work visa. We have just got to wait and see if universities use this to attract poor students who have to take a loan to pay the fees and work in unskilled jobs for two years to pay it back.

POST-1992 UNIVERSITIES CAUGHT OUT

In 2011, under the Labour government's regulations and points-based system, Glasgow Caledonian University (GCU) had its rights to sponsor international students suspended. For a number of years they had run a BA nursing (professional development) course, which had been designed to allow nursing professionals working in nursing convert the old state registered nurse (SRN) qualification and state enrolled nurse (SEN) qualification to an undergraduate degree.

However, this was a diminishing pool, as from 2013 all new nurses in the profession had to have a degree. Someone at GCU had a bright idea which would allow them to continue with significant numbers on the programme and make money.

They enrolled nurses from the Philippines onto third year of their degree.

As this was a so-called professional development degree, the students spent most of their time working in care homes. This was ideal; the university only had to teach the students two days a month and took the overseas fee. The care homes got qualified staff – as the students already had nursing diplomas from the Philippines. And the students got the chance to work in the UK legally. Or so they thought. However, the immigration rules stated that international students studying in the UK could only legally work for 20 hours a week. And that was before the points-based system and sponsorship was introduced.

There were 150 Filipino students on the programme, representing a significant income to the university. When sponsorship came along, they continued with the programme after all it had been in breach of the previous visa regulations and no one had bothered then – so why would the new regulations make any difference?

Apart from the hours that the students worked, with the new regulations, the university had to show that they were ensuring the students attended classes, they knew where they were staying and there was a minimum attendance requirement to ensure the students were full time.

In this one programme GCU had multiple breaches of the sponsorship regulations. After suspension, GCU accepted a slap on the wrist and promised not to do it again and they were reinstated – the nurses had to leave the country, leaving old folk all over the UK wondering where that nice Filipino nurse had gone. GCU was the only university to have its sponsorship suspended under Labour's points-based system but others were given the chance to clean up their acts in numerous ways.

With Theresa Mays intention to reduce international student numbers from 2012, things began to heat up. By 2014, a further five post-1992 universities had fallen foul of the regulations designed to allow only the brightest and best into the UK.

Almost immediately, under the new May regulation, in February 2012, Teesside University had its HTS revoked. What was worrying for all universities about this was that the suspension was over 'administrative issues' rather than any serious breach. The UKBA said that they had found issues with student records that needed 'clarification' (UK Visa Bureau 2012). Teesside quickly resolved the issues but UKBA had taken them off the list of sponsors, negatively affecting the £15.3 million in tuition fees that the university relied on. This suspension over processes rather than deliberate flaunting of regulations put the fear of God into the university sector.

In 2012, a serious and more deliberate breach of regulations was discovered in London Met University. The UKBA cited 'failure to address serious and systematic failings' as being the reason. Damian Green told the BBC that a 'significant proportion' of students did not have a good standard of English and there was no proof that half of those sampled were turning up for lectures (BBC 2012).

He said, 'What we found here is a serious systemic failure where it appears that the university doesn't have the capacity to be a proper sponsor and to have confidence that the students coming have the right to be here in the first place' (BBC 2012).

Unfortunately, no one had really worked out the consequences of withdrawing sponsorship. While London Met complained of the processes – they claimed that they had only found out they had lost their status from an article in the *Sunday Times* – the Home Office tried to work out what to do with the 2,600 students at London Met who no longer had valid visas, some of whom had so far done two years of study and paid significant fees. The Home Office talked about sending the students home and the universities minister David Willets announced the formation of a task force to help affected students. They had 60 days to find a new sponsor or leave the country. In a feeding frenzy, other universities grabbed the students and fees leaving a substantial hole in London Met's finances.

It wasn't the first time for the university. In 2008 it had been announced that the London Met had been under-reporting its dropout rates and over-recruiting students above its quota. Higher Education Funding Council (HEFC) was threatening to claw back £56 million it had overpaid the university. The then principal resigned immediately, but kept taking his salary for another six months – a perfect example of how toothless post-1992 universities' boards of governors are. Whether this shortfall in funding was the reason that the university had enrolled so many unsuitable students at the risk of its sponsorship status or the university had a culture of risk-taking is hard to say.

In April 2013, London Met's license was reinstated. But given the worldwide publicity, London Met's reputation overseas was tarnished, and recruitment was a fraction of what it had been. London Met took the UKBA to court over how it had managed the process and there was an out-of-court settlement.

While these high-profile cases sent shivers through the university and colleges sector, there were still some who felt that the fees from international students was worth the risk.

In 2014, a further three post-1992 universities fell foul of UKBA and it was the tricky English language problem that did for them. A panorama investigation into a SELT uncovered another English language college scam. The Test of English for International Communication (TOEIC) was US-run and had been recognised by UKBA as being a SELT. However, BBC's Panorama (BBC 2014a) found out that for £500, in a number of colleges which had been approved by the owners of TOEIC to run the test, one would be guaranteed a pass. They filmed undercover footage showing a student making her way to a secure computer terminal linked up to a government-approved testing. But minutes before the exam was due to start, new people entered the room. In the footage, the dozen or so candidates in the room were seen standing aside from their desks to allow these 'fake sitters' to sit in their places and take the exam for them.

At another multiple-choice exam in the centre a few days later, the invigilator was seen simply reading out the answers to all 200 questions so the registered candidates can copy them down. A two-hour test took just seven minutes to complete. All in all, it was calculated that there were 29,000 invalid test scores discovered and 19,000 questionable ones.

The Panorama investigation also managed to buy fake bank account details through the college to show immigration officials they had enough funds for a visa. And this was after Theresa May's stricter measures to stop bogus colleges.

The owners of the colleges were eventually prosecuted, but there were consequences for a number of post-1992 universities who had accepted students with the fake English language results.

Glyndwr University had its HTS suspended. It was calculated that there were 350 students with questionable English language scores. A spokesman for the university expressed annoyance that it had been put in this position. He said, 'We have partnerships with a number of suppliers and are incredibly disappointed to have been the subject of any deception or activity that would put that licence under threat. To be put in this position by external partners is frustrating as Glyndwr University takes its responsibility as a Highly Trusted Sponsor very seriously' (BBC 2014a).

By calling the partner 'a supplier', the spokesman gave away the manner in which Glyndwr was operating, with students being seen as goods. But then as the THES reported, a 'String of poor decisions preceded suspension of highly trusted status', and go on to catalogue that in 2012–14 the university had a deficit of £4 million. The cash holdings had 'plummeted from nearly £3 million to £141,000, while its current liabilities were greater than its current assets' and the university had asked for an overdraft (Mathews 2014). These were due to the principal and executive of the university being involved in speculative spending such as buying a company that made optical lenses for the European Telescope and a dog track that was rented out to Wrexham Football Club – where were the board of governors? Once again there was a direct link between financial need and the level of risk taken when recruiting foreign students.

The University of Bedford and University of West London were also warned by UKBA that they would be suspended until they had been investigated. These universities were the only ones that had official warnings. There were many others that have had unofficial warnings to clean up their act that have not appeared in the papers. No pre-1992 university that has been censured by the UKBA, let alone lost its HTS.

LONDON CAMPUSES

UK university staff attending recruitment events and talking to students all over the world are constantly asked how far their campus is from London. Apart from fanatical Manchester United supporters, or deluded Glasgow Rangers fans, London is the big draw for international students coming to the UK. No amount of claiming that it is only an hour away, then sotto voice 'by plane' is likely to fool modern students.

So rather than pretend that your university is in London, why not move it there?

With this thought, universities in provincial cities, not considered to be attractive to international students, rented, bought or borrowed premises in London, which they called their London campus.

It was specifically at its London campus that Glyndwr had been found to be most negligent. It was to make the financial targets of its London campus that they had enrolled 350 students with limited English. And so when Glyndwr was given back its licence, it was under new strict conditions. They had to close down their London campus, which had over 2,000 of the 2,600 international students that Glyndwr recruited.

When announcing this, James Brokenshire, the minister for security and immigration highlighted that abuse was happening in the London sub-campuses of other UK Universities but they were allowed to retain their sponsorship status. He said, 'Other universities are involved in the continuing investigation, and further action may follow, although because of the steps they have already taken to improve their processes, including voluntarily ceasing overseas recruitment to London sub-campuses, we will not at this stage remove their right to sponsor foreign students' (UK Parliament Hansard 2014).

Brokenshire asked the Quality Assurance Agency (QAA) to examine the London campuses to see whether any further action should be taken against parent institutions. In the case of London campuses, the QAA was directed by the minister to do more than only look at whether these London outposts were ticking the QAA boxes. It was to look at 'causes for concern'.

The report titled, 'London Campuses of UK Universities: Overview Report of a Thematic Enquiry by the Quality Assurance Agency for Higher Education' (QAA 2014), which was published on 17 December 2014, found that there were 8,400 students studying in London sub-campuses. Two were pre-1992 universities but the majority 11 out of 13 were post-1992. The two pre-1992 universities that had campuses open at the time of the report, Liverpool and Ulster, had opened later than most of the pre-1992 universities.

This shows a recurring pattern, where post-1992 universities are not alone in developing innovative but risky schemes to increase numbers, but they are in the majority and at the forefront of such developments.

It was apparent from the report that these campuses had one raison d'être – fees from international students. The QAA review stated as much: 'Most of the London campuses were established between 2009 and 2014. The main reason was to increase the recruitment of international students who would be more attracted to London than to the home campus. Student numbers on these campuses range from under 100 to over 2,000, with the average being 652 students' (QAA 2014).

It wasn't as if the government had suddenly decided that there were not enough university places in London and begged universities from Scotland to Wales to come down and help out.

These universities weren't there for the common weal or to enrich the lives of UK students or local industry; they were purely and utterly business ventures. And as business ventures, they were run fundamentally different from the main university campus

Like English language schools before them, they opened in the capital to make a quick buck. Any talk of a university community was irrelevant, any chance of intermingling with local students or of interdisciplinary working was not possible. They ran a selected few programmes that were most in demand overseas and required the smallest resources to deliver. So the London campuses offered mainly postgraduate programmes in business, management, accountancy, tourism, law and computing (QAA 2014).

As entities set up specifically to contribute funding back to the central university coffers, they had challenging targets. Even with a London campus it was a hard sell for universities at the bottom end of the league tables as the review showed.

The *Times Higher* claimed that the QAA had been happy with the performance of the London campuses. 'QAA inquiry says London campuses not ripe for visa fraud. An inquiry has appeared to dismiss claims that student visa abuse is taking place at London branch campuses' was the headline (Grove 2014). But this was only the beginning of the report, the part where the QAA always tries to be positive. In this section the QAA review had found that the universities were 'diligent in approval and validation processes, and conscientious in their ongoing monitoring and review of programmes at their London campuses' (QAA 2014).

But the detail from the body of the report was much more meaty and quite shocking. They may have been conscientious in validations, monitoring and review. but they were taking students onto the programmes based on their financial qualifications rather than academic. The following extract from the report shows that the reviewers identified:

> problems and potential risks in relation to admission processes. In one case the university placed recruitment in the hands of a private organisation which subcontracted to agents in different countries and led to a lack of control on admissions. At another campus, students were admitted when not appropriately qualified for their programmes. International qualifications were not aligned with UK qualifications; and students were accepted from a private UK organisation whose Home Office licence had been revoked. Also, the applications provided no evidence of relevant attainment, nor had they been translated into English. One campus had to provide emergency pre-registration language teaching to remedy the students' lack of appropriate qualifications. Another has relied on two major recruitment providers, but owing to concerns about the poor quality of some applications has terminated an agreement with one agency and is now moving towards developing its own online student recruitment and agent management system. (QAA 2014)

Some of these behaviours no doubt helped students gain visas fraudulently. It is an example of how, when there is money involved, some universities lose sight of their primary mission. This behaviour was restricted to foreign students until the fee cap was increased to £9,000, after which, as the Augar Review (Augar 2019) revealed, similar sharp practices were introduced for home students. The report further stated:

> Universities are aware that the attainment and completion rates of students on their London campuses may not match those of their counterparts on the main campuses. This they generally attribute to the admission of students with lower entry qualifications than on comparable programme at the home institution, though there is some evidence that the quality of learning resources and support is a contributory factor. (QAA 2014)

After Glyndwr's London campus was shut down, the remaining campuses of other universities were given a quiet word and they quickly realigned their admissions procedures to be the same as their home campuses, causing an immediate downturn in numbers.

CHAPTER 8

INTERNATIONAL RECRUITMENT: ECONOMIC SUCCESS VERSUS TENSIONS AT HOME

INTERNATIONAL ACTIVITIES CHANGE UNIVERSITIES

From the late 1990s on, heads of international recruitment with a small team of staff and willing academics to run about the world morphed into directors of international colleges or deans, pro-vice chancellors and vice principals of internationalisation, global engagement or world domination. What was a small cottage industry, on the periphery, barely noticeable to staff on the front lines, became the beating heart of the university. A measure of how important international business is now to post-1992 universities can be seen in the makeup of their senior staff teams.

Of the 31 original post-1992 universities still in existence, 21 have senior staff who are members of the university executive team with responsibility solely for international activities.

Five of these are deputy vice chancellors with the majority being pro-vice chancellors. Most have an academic background, all but two appear to have migrated from academic posts as their faculties and universities became more active overseas, rather than having an academic background in international education or international business. Only three seem to have no substantial background as academic staff – coming up through the international recruitment route. Interestingly, two of the three non-academic senior staff are in two of the three Scottish universities that gained their charter in 1992. In addition, many have senior staff usually in the role of assistant/associate/ deputy deans in faculties with international responsibility as their main area of work.

A FINANCIAL SUCCESS STORY

It is not a surprise as it is big business. The UK attracts the second largest number of international students second only to the much larger United States. In 2014–15 some 438,000 students came to study in the UK with a value to the UK economy estimated at £25.8 billion (Oxford Economics 2017).

In a briefing report commissioned by Universities UK, it was estimated that international students paid £4.8 billion in tuition fees to UK universities. The report went on to calculate the economic impact of international students on the wider UK economy and found the following:

1. As well as university fees and accommodation, international students spent £5.4 billion off-campus on goods and services

2. Spending by international students supported 206,600 jobs all over the UK

3. Visitors to international students in the UK spent an estimated £520 million – benefitting in particular the transport, hotels, hospitality, cultural, recreational and sports attraction sectors – generating an estimated knock-on impact of £1 billion in gross output

4. Taking their university payments, off-campus spending and the spending of their visitors together, international students generated £25.8 billion in gross output

5. International students were responsible for £10.8 billion of UK export earnings

6. The economic activity and employment sustained by international students' off campus spending generated £1 billion tax revenues. This is the equivalent to the salaries of 31,700 nurses or 25,000 police officers (Oxford Economics 2017).

7. In addition, many post-1992 universities bring in significant income from teaching their programmes overseas, for example, transnational education (TNE). It was estimated that TNE generated revenues of £496 million in 2012–13.

The above report was of course commissioned by Universities UK as part of a number of briefing papers on the value of UK universities. They were intended to influence the government at a time when it was outlining a new industrial Strategy and Britain was leaving the EU. The Universities UK report concludes that 'any government strategies for economic success should recognise the fundamental importance of EU and non-EU international students'.

EU FEES INCOME

The argument about the financial benefits from EU students is particularly interesting. In 2016–17 there were 134,000 EU students studying in UK universities. A Universities UK report entitled, 'International Education Facts and Figures', brought out before the referendum in 2016, estimated that EU students contributed £3.7 billion to the UK economy and supported 34,000 jobs. But, of course, this was a paper designed to show how leaving the EU would cause problems – it didn't show how it came to calculate those figures. In particular, EU students are entitled to student loans to pay their fees, which have been shown to be heavily subsidised by the tax payer as it is expected that at least 40 per cent will never be paid back. For EU students, this is most probably higher and thus no doubt harder to get student loan repayment from a graduate paying tax in Europe than one employed in England.

While much positive spin in the media concentrated on financial success, in academia they tried hard to justify the case for international recruitment on social, political and academic terms.

From polytechnics with 6 per cent of their student population from overseas and the majority from the local area, new universities have changed dramatically (Pratt 1997). Not only have they become much larger but have also become international in terms of students and staff. Universities UK Patterns and Trends in UK Higher Education 2018 (Universities UK 2018) showed that in 2016–17, 30 per cent of academics in the UK are international.

The success of international recruitment was such that by 2016–17, the UK higher education sector had 19.1 per cent of students from outside the UK. But these were neither evenly geographically spread nor indeed evenly spread by discipline. Business schools in the UK had on an average 36.5 per cent non-EU students; engineering and technology students made up 31.8 per cent. Nearly one-third of non-EU students were from China (21 per cent of all non-UK students) and 42 per cent of all postgraduate students were from outwith the UK (Universities UK 2018).

In post-1992 universities that recruited a large number of students into advanced years of undergraduate programmes, it was not unusual to have students who had been with all-British cohorts in a business school programme to arrive back from summer break to find they were outnumbered by new international students, many of who required extensive academic, cultural and language assistance.

This is not restricted to post-1992 universities, but post-1992 universities are considered to be recruiting universities as opposed to selecting universities and so have less control over the programmes they offer and the countries they recruit in, if they have the aim of maximising income.

Postgraduate programmes are run for almost fully international cohorts and can close down when a market collapses, as did the Indian market after new visa regulations.

In the same way, EU students are used to prop up programmes where there are not enough home students to fill quotas, because EU students count as home students.

INTERNATIONAL RECRUITMENT

The British Council

The British Council is in effect the government's arm for cultural relations (although it is a non-departmental public body). Its role is to promote wider understanding of the UK and its culture and to promote the English language overseas. It used to focus on screening films, lectures and exhibitions, or taking groups of spies disguised as Morris dancers to Russia, pipe bands to Colombia and farmers from the Lake District to Australia to run demonstrations on drystane dyking. The British Council is a sort of unisex global women's institute, which during the cold war was a hot bed of spies and counterintelligence operators.

This would explain the reason why many heads of mission even to this day are graduates of the old school – charming men or women, who seem to be somewhat bemused with the way the world works. They change their posting every three years and it is always easy to see the stage in their posting they are at. In the first year they are learning a new language and culture and constantly hark back with nostalgia to their previous posting. By the second year they are getting the hang of things, know the people and are just beginning to develop some meaningful relationships. Then comes the third year where they are applying for the next posting, getting involved in politics back home to make sure they don't get sent to Afghanistan or in fact any bloody 'stan.

Since the 1990s, as well as managing the British Brand, the British Council has increasingly been forced into an internal commercial war. Each mission has to attract as much business as possible and they had to charge for their services.

The magnificent buildings that had once been deemed necessary to show the UK's status as a super power have been sold off and the British Council offices moved out of the embassies into smaller, but still smart, corporate buildings.

Now education is the biggest business for them, from selling English language training to pimping universities.

But first they have to sell the country they are posted in, to the universities back home. It's a circle. Report after report is generated by missions throughout the 200 countries where the British Council has a mission. The job of the report is to show that their country is the next big thing for investment – to entice the universities and other investors in, like wasps to a jar of jam. Funded by PMI, the British Council provides a wealth of market information. From market intelligence briefs, global trends analyses, student insights, horizon scanning, inside guides to help universities penetrate new markets – all use the language of commerce and trade.

Universities' international strategies are developed using the material provided by the British Council. They now talk in a language previously foreign to university academics, key performance indicators, B-to-B relationships, brand identity, market share, market image, market penetration, target audience, influencing the influencers, unique selling propositions and so on. These are bandied about like fairy dust to make it all seem considered, and almost scientific – in its complexity. But the reality is that no two organisations take the same data from the British Council and come to the same conclusion as to a strategy. One will see an opportunity in the fact that there are no students from a country currently studying in the UK. Others will see the largest markets as the only place to expend effort, some others will decide that these are too mature and look elsewhere. Some, usually academic departments with an enthusiast in charge of international recruitment, will run about the world amassing air miles and little else. But all this can be justified if you look hard enough at the tons of information spewed out by the British Council, HESA, Universities UK International Group, the Observatory on Borderless Education, the International Student Barometer, and these are just some of the sources. One thing academics are good at is interpreting data and presenting a case for spending money

As well as selling the country to UK universities, the British Council has to sell UK higher education to the country. But they are somewhat handicapped by the premises of a single sector developed by PMI. To this day because of the tyranny of the brand, British Council workers overseas have to sell higher education as a single sector. This must be hard. It's a bit like the French selling their whole food and drinks sector as world class. No difference between the oldest three-star Michelin restaurant Paul Bocuse and the fast food chain Quick. They are all part of the world-class food sector! Add to this the fact that Scottish undergraduate degrees are four years rather than the three in England and you can see how difficult they must find it.

It doesn't bother the really world-class universities; they spend more time and effort rejecting students than courting them. But for lowly ranked universities being embraced in the arms of a brand which claims they are world class is priceless.

The brand and therefore the British Council have to ignore the fact that, by almost all measures, many UK universities are quite definitely not world class – but then, why should they be? So, according to the British Council website, UK universities are the best in the world – all of them! All use the most up-to-date technology and top the world league tables. As the BC website says:

> The UK's academic reputation is world-renowned. Built on a heritage that is now centuries old, our approach to education applies the very latest learning theory through universities that routinely top international tables. (British Council 2018)

The British Council website goes on to talk of the UK's 162 higher education institutions as being 'all held to strict standards by the government, so you know you are getting the best teaching, support and resources available' (British Council 2018). It is unclear which branch of government is responsible for holding universities to these strict standards. The QAA is a self-regulated organisation and has admitted that it does not have a role in ensuring standards of UK university qualifications (HMI 1989). With the change in the fee cap, the government has left the size and shape of universities solely to market forces and exert little influence.

And, as for research, every university is included.

> We're ranked second in the world for science and research and 54 per cent of our output is world-leading. Our field-weighted citation impact is higher than the US, Canada, Germany, Japan and Brazil, so when you study here *you can be sure* you'll be working alongside some of the best minds – and using some of the best technology – in the world. (British Council 2018)

So that's it. It's a fact – according to the British Council, when you study business studies in a post-1992 university not even ranked in the top 1,000 universities in the world by the THES rankings, you are studying in a system that's centuries old, using the latest learning technology, conducting world-leading research and working with the best minds in the world!

But the British Council is not just about managing the brand; for many years the main interaction that UK universities had with the British Council in-country were through recruitment fairs.

RECRUITMENT FAIRS

Recruitment fairs are a mixture of a meat market and a beauty contest. In fact one fair that used to be held in Brunei was in a hall that was next door to the halal slaughter house and smelt just like a meat market, as the air conditioning sucked in the foul odour of dead animals and disgorged it into the hall. The most popular fairs are organised by the British Council and bounce about the world from city to city and country to country. They all follow a similar pattern. The day before the fair opens, university staff set up their stands in the hall, which at that point does not bother switching on its air conditioning as they are only the hired help. That evening there is an opening ceremony where the ambassador or some such worthy show that an Oxbridge education really is worthwhile, by introducing themselves in the local lingo before giving a speech straight out of the brand guidelines, 'World class, traditional but modern, surprisingly affordable'. Meanwhile the five star hotel that the event is being held in circulate an amuse bouche take on local street food, and most importantly wine and beer that is free and free flowing!

When highly ranked pre-1992 universities bother attending fairs, they do so to give information to prospective and existing applicants, meet alumni and dignitaries, explain to others why they were rejected and have a jolly nice time.

Not so post-1992 universities and lowly ranked pre-1992 universities that for years made on-the-spot offers to applicants. In many cases the international recruitment team was given the power to do this; in others, specially picked academics would come to the fair. Some even gave the recruitment staff, who were attending fairs, targets for the amount of offers made rather than how many students actually were recruited.

It was not unusual in those days to see students going from university stand to university stand to show the offer the competition had made and try to get a better deal, either cheaper or entry to a more advanced year. With just about every university in the UK represented at the biggest fairs, the level of competition meant that there was a race to the bottom. After all, each student nabbed was worth around £10,000 a year minus discounts and agents' fees, of course.

This changed with the introduction of university sponsorship for visas and particularly Highly Trusted Status (HTS).

One measure as to whether one lost HTS was the percentage of unsuccessful applications for visas from each university. At first it was said that if 2 per cent of students you had made an offer to and given a sponsorship number to were refused visas then your HTS was in danger. This turned out to be scaremongering and the rejection rate was set at 10 per cent.

Even so, the notion of spraying about offers in the hope that some students actually arrived was no longer viable. On-the-spot offers were much reduced as there had to be serious checks made before any offer would be risked, and with the new system where students were given a unique number that the university was given from the Home Office meant they could no longer get multiple offers.

HOW THE FAIRS WORK

Each university hires a stand which consists of a box with a table in front of which the university lays out its wares. In the 1990s this was simple fare, a tartan cloth for Scottish universities, or a cloth with the universities logo or crest spread over the table. On top of it some shiny printed material, a prospectus or some details of the programmes of study, some pictures of the university or visions of ye olde England were stuck onto walls behind the table and some goodies designed to tempt student to spend their families' life savings strewn over the table. Perhaps a piece of Kendal mint cake or a bar of Tablet, or for the more sophisticated, a fridge magnet, a plastic bag and a pen with the university's logo or any other such tacky cheap and light gift. Tat made in Asia was flown back to its country of origin to be distributed to the grateful natives.

By the turn of the century and beyond, the advertising material became more sophisticated. The actual backing for the stand now comes in various shaped geodetic frames, which makes the plastic printed advertising three dimensional, the promotional video, previously a CD displayed on the overhead TV, is now displayed on a tablet chained to the leg of the table. But the tacky gifts remain the same.

No one believes these gifts make any difference, it just gives staff managing the stand something to do when confronted with someone who quite obviously has just popped in to get out of the monsoon or to bask in the glamour of so many top foreign universities visiting their city – give them a pen, some publicity material and a plastic bag and smile politely until a real prospect comes along. Or alternatively, when standing around waiting for someone to talk to, the exhibiter can look at their competitors' gifts, or rearrange their own in a pleasing pattern like an exotic bird trying to impress a partner.

And when one does approach, you need to pounce. The gold standard is a student who has government funding already in place – for most post-1992 universities, these are rare beasts indeed.

THE STAFF

As you can imagine, with free drinks at receptions every second night and the freedom of being away from home, the hundreds of exhibiters behave no better than would be expected. There are two distinct groups: the international recruitment staff – salespeople, often single, always young, enthusiastic, target driven – and the academics, mostly middle aged, often recently divorced or soon-to-be divorced, for some reason wanting away from the office. For the former, it is a career and for the latter, a chance to party at someone else's expense.

There is always a risk when asking a head of department to recommend an academic to accompany the recruitment team, especially if you are requiring an engineer or scientist. What is required is someone preferably young, personable and able to make small talk and quick decisions. Not a description of too many academics. In general, academics on recruitment trips come in a variety of types.

The old hippy: They turn up to the airport with shorts, sandals, a Hawaiian shirt and an old battered rucksack. They stand unhelpfully regaling the poor international officer, struggling with the paraphernalia needed for two weeks' fair, going on about how they don't know why anyone would need more than one carry-on bag and sharing stories of their travels back in the day. On the morning of the fair recruitment, the staff get a phone call from the academic's room. Thank goodness the room has a phone beside the toilet, as the academic, white-faced and weak-voiced explains that the street food they had eaten the night before, despite warnings not too, had in fact incapacitated them. They couldn't understand it – in all their travels when they were 18 years old, this had never happened

The recent divorcee or about-to-be divorced: Mostly male, they hit the bar in the airport, attend all the receptions, hovering up as much free wine as they can in the two hours allotted, then hit the town. Hard Rock Cafes are standard venues, where their egos are massaged by young girls whose jobs it is to encourage excessive drinking. For the price of a 'cocktail' that looks and tastes exactly like Coca-Cola, a girl sits beside them and asks in broken English, 'where you from', smiling vacantly at the reply and topping up the academic's beer.

Or for those that know where to find them, they go to bars where expats of a similar age play darts and drink beer from home, telling jokes that would have been considered racists in the 1970s and behaving in a misogynistic way not condoned in the UK since Victorian times.

Some embarrassingly follow the young international staff, from the reception on to what they still called a discotheques, where they are hit on by beautiful tall women with sexy deep voices and scarves around their prominent Adam's apples.

By the time the fair starts, they are a shadow of their former selves. White faced, smelling of stale beer, they sit very gently down hoping no one will talk to them, wondering if there is a reception that night and whether anyone saw them sneaking loudly and drunkenly into the hotel – not alone.

The pragmatic academic: These usually come from schools or faculties that are heavily reliant on income or numbers from overseas. They are keen to take any student and willing to bend the rules and put their signature on any application that passes the mirror test. Put a mirror in front of an applicant and if it steams up they get a place, some even go for a temperature test so they can get the recently dead as well. The only problem they cause recruitment staff is when the students arrive in the class and the people teaching them blame those buggers in international recruitment.

The budget holder: Heads of departments, deans or higher. They fly out separately from the recruitment staff, as they believe in equality and don't think it right for them to be on the same plane, and turn left into business class when the other staff turn right into economy. So they take a plane out by themselves. But only when the recruitment fair goes to a city that is interesting. Not for them the drag of manning a stand or talking to students. They are there for the reception, meeting partners, doing big business – swimming, snorkelling, sightseeing.

Recruitment staff see them as a mixed bag. They can be hard work, expecting to be treated with the respect they feel they deserve. But outwith their empire, they are accessible, and if sucked up to, they might be helpful in the future – some even turn out to be pleasant company. But importantly, they have a budget and are willing to put things on expenses that mere mortals wouldn't dream of.

THE BIGGEST

For years the biggest and best fair was the Malaysian fair. Nearly every university in the UK joined, together with some boarding schools, a few private English language providers and a small number of further education colleges. All bought stands from the British Council. In its heyday, there were over two hundred exhibiters.

Back in the day, all the real business was done on the mainland, Kuala Lumpur (KL) and Penang. But after a week of hard work, selling the university to prospective students, making offers, wining and dining agents, the recruitment team had made the money for the university and deserved a bit of a break.

So those in the know went on to the two bonus fairs in Borneo. One in Kuching and one in Kota Kinabalu. There they recruited the grandsons and granddaughters of head hunters and pillow dictionaries who, as bumiputeras, were given funding to be educated in Scunthorpe and on the banks of the Tyne.

In Kuching the fair was held in the Hilton. Normally Hiltons would be considered somewhat downmarket for the university set, but the views from the Hilton in Kuching are some of the most spectacular in the world. Certainly one of the most beautiful of any Hilton. The coffee-brown Sarawak River flows serpent-like through the city centre. It is as if it was designed by an oriental Capability Brown just so that the guests in the Hilton glass-walled executive lounge would have the best views. Small slim crafts with low roofs painted in yellow with the Lipton's tea logo in red, ferry passengers across to the side of the river where the Istana sits on a hill. The Istana was built by one of the Rajah Brookes. A line of Brits extending from James Brookes, an English 'adventurer' who had been given Sarawak and all its people as a gift for using his superior weapons on the right side of a war that was none of his business. He reinstated the Sultan of Brunei on his throne and was given Sarawak, a small country of his very own to rule over. The Brookes family ruled until just after the Second World War, when they gifted the country to the Federated states of Malaya.

In Kuching, the recruitment fair lasted for one, not very busy, day and then on to the beaches of Kota Kinabalu (KK) in Sabah where it was held in the Shangri La Tanjun Aru resort – an idyllic spot set in a national park with 47 coral islands. There, the fair lasted a morning, usually a Friday, despite the fact that it is the Muslim holy day, so that those that had paid the British Council for stands had the chance to stay over the weekend. At that point in the fair there was a surprisingly large number of senior staff, given that there was almost no business in KK.

It was such a stunning place that one principal of a Scottish ex-polytechnic flew out every year with his wife to be debriefed by his director of international recruitment. We know this as it was mentioned in his sacking for, among a number of other things, nepotism and taking foreign trips with 'holiday elements'.

In a bizarre twist after the university had employed a new principal, a tribunal judged that the university court had not followed procedure and that he should be reinstated. So for a short time, the university was paying two principals until it appealed the appeal and won the case.

With the change in visa systems, students could no longer get on-the-spot offers and negotiate a good deal at the fair, and attendance dropped. In 2018 there were only 45 institutions attending the Malaysian fair and it is now held for one afternoon in KL only.

AGENTS

One of the most common ways of attracting students for UK universities is through agents. These are commercial companies that actively recruit students on behalf of large numbers of competing universities from competing countries.

They usually have multiple offices in country, can speak the language, have links to in-country schools, colleges and universities and often the MOE. They have an in-depth knowledge of the educational landscape and are seen as an invaluable tool for recruitment; 38 per cent of international students in the UK are recruited through agents. The most well-known agents in a country often have to be wooed by post-1992 universities who are low in the league tables and may refuse to represent them. This leads post-1992 universities in a more precarious position than better-known universities and more likely to work with less well-established players. Or be more willing to pay larger commission to bigger agencies.

To ameliorate the risk involved in allowing a private organisation to represent the university, complex contracts have been designed mainly to say that these agents aren't actually your official representatives. These contracts have clauses to protect the universities' reputation from bad behaviour by the overseas agent. But presumably, the lawyers who wrote the contracts were unaware of the World Justice Projects Rule of Law Index or the Corruption Perception Index. If they were, they could easily understand just how little signing a contract means in certain countries.

But much of it is show – to show that the university tried to control a private company working thousands of miles away.

So if some less reputable agents actually advertised in the local language – telling the natives of the beauty of ancient Milton Keynes, the London suburb of Paisley, the world-class and famous Metropolitan University of Nuneaton – the best university in the UK, the university has an out – the agent had promised they wouldn't do that – and in writing too.

When the agents entice potential students into their offices situated above hairdressers salons and shop lots, the hard sell begins – or as the universities prefer it – the in-depth counselling session which helps guide potential students towards the best option for their particular circumstances.

Unattractive new universities, near the bottom of the league tables based in an unknown British city, have to ensure that they are at the forefront of these completely unbiased so-called consultations. So they invite the counsellors on fully paid trips to the UK, Bangkok or Beijing for an agents' conference. These typically include banquets, sightseeing and large presents. The most successful develop incentive schemes which make agents very rich if they send students to their university. Agents are often given stipends for marketing. Some have a close enough relationship with a specific university that they have a dedicated office and staff for that university – paid for by the university, of course. The whole plan is to ensure that any student that you would take is directed to your university. It does not matter if the programme is most suitable – whether it will be value for money and help the student achieve their life ambitions – or if the student could have a choice of several universities and programmes. No one questions the moral of this situation. Whole families' life savings are invested in an education overseas sold by a completely biased commercial entity whose sole motive is profit. And UK universities climb over each other to make sure that their offering is most profitable to these companies.

Such competition means that there is always the danger of escalating costs to institutions. Agents claiming they have been given a better deal from competitors push up the commission – of course, you would only increase commission rates if you believe that the agent is only motivated by money rather than wanting the best for their clients.

Data from British institutions reported in *Inside Higher Education* suggest that, on average, UK universities paid £1,782 in agent commission fees per student recruited in 2013/14, compared with an estimated £981 per student in 2010/11 (Havergal 2015). But these are average figures; for many post-1992 universities, the figures will no doubt be higher. In addition, the article by Havergal said that the 106 out of 158 institutions that replied to a FOI request in 2013 spent £86 million on agents' fees.

In 2010 a new Bribery Act was enacted. The act created 'a new offence under section 7 which can be committed by commercial organisations which fail to prevent persons associated with them from committing bribery on their behalf. It is a full defence for an organisation to prove that despite a particular case of bribery it nevertheless had adequate procedures in place to prevent persons associated with it from bribing'. In effect, if an overseas agent is caught bribing an official, the signatory of a commercial contract with that agent could be imprisoned unless one could show that there were procedures in place to prevent bribery. Universities rushed to develop questionnaires for agents, carry out due diligence and tick the boxes that the government required. Senior staff fought to get their name off the list of those who could sign off agent's contracts. But not much really changed.

Until 2010 entry standards were at risk through the use of agents. Before the advent of HTS, many allowed so-called 'trusted' agents to make admission decisions. Surprisingly, agents getting paid per student, who were allowed to make the decision on entry to the university, were very flexible in their interpretation of entry levels and English language proficiency. But they did provide large numbers of students, and it was the job of junior academics to teach them not the dean who had signed the contract.

In the sector there has been some debate about the way in which UK universities use and rely on agents. As private organisations there is no real control over their behaviour in-country. However, the debate around the use of agents has focused on how to control the agents. There has been little debate around whether the hard sell that agents carry out is ethical or in the interest of the student. As far as they are concerned, they are employing agents to sell their universities and the fact that there may be another university or course that is more suitable for that student should not be mentioned. In some countries such as China, there is a strict registration scheme for agents, but in most this is not the case. Rather than have a debate around the ethics and potential risks of using agents, the British Council found a way of making money out of them. In 2006 they introduced a training scheme for agents and an ethical code of practice. Agents who paid for and completed the online training and signed up for the code of practice were placed on a database of the British Council Accredited Agents. Universities could be safe in the knowledge that the agent they were employing could afford to pay for the training and registration.

CHAPTER 9

INTERNATIONALISATION

The dramatic change in student communities in the UK, Australia and to some extent North America from the late 1990s was a laboratory sitting at the feet of academics in educational and social sciences. Leading researchers in international education such as Jane Knight, Hans De Witt, Simon Marginson and any amount of international support staff studying part time for a doctor of business administration (DBA) documented, rationalised and explained motivations, actions and results of international activities carried out by the sector.

These academics not only described what was happening but gave a whole new language for international staff to use. Directors of international recruitment became directors of internationalisation who wrote strategies about academic, social and political drivers to internationalisation, or being somewhere along a journey from symbolic internationalisation to transformational integrated internationalisation, but failed to mention the real commercial drivers. These strategies claimed to realise that internationalisation was not just about international student recruitment but could embrace the whole university community and be embedded in everything the university did. Money was no longer mentioned in these new strategies, it was like the elephant in the room, the emperor's new clothes, the fart in the lift. Everyone knew about it, but was too polite to mention it, let alone stand up proudly and say that the strategy was to make as much money as possible.

But the truth is while there were elements of internationalisation that developed throughout all universities as a reaction to the increasingly international student body, the motivations behind it were in reality financial and these motives are in fact a barrier to internationalisation of home students.

The UK governments, including the devolved Parliament of Scotland, as demonstrated in previous chapters, had little interest in internationalisation as a process of integrating an international, intercultural, or global dimension into the purpose, functions or delivery of postsecondary education.

They were interested in fees to make up for a funding gap. And the place where that funding gap was most critical was in post-1992 universities. So it is not surprising that any notion of internationalisation as an integrated whole in these universities has always been secondary to the commercial imperatives of recruiting more full-fee-paying students.

The reality that for the whole sector, commercialisation had hijacked internationalisation was recognised in an article in the University World News on 12 October 2018 where Jane Knight and Hans De Witt asked, 'What contribution has internationalisation made to HE?'

They point out that, for most institutions, internationalisation is a group of fragmented and unrelated activities throughout organisations. In post-1992 universities the most high-profile and best resourced of these activities is international recruitment which causes problems as pointed out in this book and recognised by Knight and De Witt:

> The increasing commodification of higher education remains primarily oriented toward reaching targets without a debate on potential risks and ethical consequences [...] Who could have forecasted that internationalisation would transform from what has been traditionally considered a process based on values of cooperation, partnership, exchange, mutual benefits and capacity building to one that is increasingly characterised by competition, commercialisation, self-interest and status building? (Knight and de Wit 2018)

Seeing international education as merely an export can disadvantage UK students. Mass recruitment of international students brings in needed funding, but is not necessarily conducive to internationalisation. Salehi-Sangari and Foster recognise that universities seek to meet a dual challenge when internationalising, first, 'to create a more internationalised student from our own university and secondly to meet the needs of international students who may be visitors on exchange or enrolled for an award, having chosen the UK as the supplier of their education' (Salehi-Sangari and Foster 1999).

INTERNATIONALISATION AT HOME

At a practical level, especially before fees were introduced for home students, universities recognised that they were open to accusations of being biased towards international students who brought in significant income. PMI2, with its emphases on ensuring that the experience of international students was good quality rather than improving the experience of the whole student body, did not help.

And there was some disquiet among academics that the only students that benefited from international recruitment were international students. As I wrote in 2006 in the magazine *Professional Engineer*, 'Given the choice between a British student who only speaks English and has a degree from a UK University and an international student who speaks two languages and often has a degree from their own country experience of different cultures and the same qualification from the UK, which one would a multinational company choose to employ?' (Brady 2006).

The notion that by recruiting international students one created an international environment for all students and home students got an international education by some sort of osmosis was argued by aggressive recruiting institutions.

But Black and any number of researchers debunked this myth when he points out that there is a danger in 'the belief that international students' presence automatically benefits home students without any further input from faculty' (Black 2004).

The reality is that the whole higher education sector failed to ensure that all home students receive an international education. As will be shown later, other countries have attempted to address this issue by developing high-level strategies which have internationalisation at home and study abroad as elements. But at a government level, UK government strategies have focused squarely on the economic benefits of international recruitment and ignored the potential to make a difference to home students. This translates directly to universities' behaviour as Anthony Welch pointed out in an article in *Higher Education*:

> The motivations for internationalisation embraced by the state are often reflected in those of institutions – and it has been noted that 'the adoption of financial goals as the major rationale by institutions and governments [...] has been shown to significantly distort programs of internationalization'. (Welch 1997)

The most recent government strategy, in 2019, was a case in point. Like its predecessors, there was a lack of any ambition in internationalisation. The 2019 strategy is set in the framework of education's contribution to the government's overall exports strategy. It's all about getting foreign students onto UK programmes. That is why it was jointly written by the Department for Education and the Department for International Trade.

Of course, nice things are said about outward mobility. But schemes to internationalise through getting UK students to study abroad have been spectacularly unsuccessful. In 2016–17 there were less than 17,000 outgoing Erasmus students, with 35 per cent of them language students (Erasmus 2017). Contrast that to 135,000 EU students and over 100,000 Chinese studying in the UK.

In the 2019 strategy, the government committed to 'continue to support' the campaign to double outbound numbers by 2020. Doubling sounds impressive, but if achieved, only 13 per cent of undergraduate students would spend some period of study abroad.

The biggest contributor to those outward mobility numbers is Erasmus, and as I write, we don't know what will happen with that. I am not sure many in the sector will feel confident with the weak statement that the government is 'open to exploring participation in the successor scheme to the current Erasmus programme' (HM Government 2019). They have been open to 'exploring' many things in the negotiations.

Outwith student outward mobility there are many examples of how international students' presence in UK universities have helped inject an international element in curriculums and programmes. The higher education academy and others provide tools, frameworks and benchmarks for internationalisation. But to internationalise you need a range of students with a geographic spread over all subject areas. When targets are set by fee intakes, this is not possible. In 2016–17, business schools in the UK had 36.5 per cent non-EU students, engineering and technology had 31.8 per cent. Nearly one-third of non-EU students were from China and 42 per cent of all postgraduate students were international. These are averages, it is not unheard of there being over 60 per cent foreign students on the final year of a business programme. Student surveys have shown that there is little integration with home students. The UK government's plan to increase international student numbers will produce graduates with cross-cultural understanding – just not British ones.

To change this, the government needs to develop an ambitious, properly funded strategy for internationalisation of home students and stop seeing international higher education as only a short-term cash cow. But it should be part of a strategy that takes in schools and other parts of society.

Internationalisation is important to the future of British industry, the education sector and society. Brexit means we must reposition ourselves in a globalised and interconnected world. We will need to make new and different connections.

CHAPTER 10

HIGH-RISK MARKETS

How do universities choose where to work? What method do they use to ensure that where they are sending staff is safe or which partnerships are morally and ethically correct?

As discussed in earlier chapters, the Prime Minister's Initiatives were firmly about how to make money from other countries by selling so-called educational services. There was no debate about whether there were moral issues around working with certain regimes. On the whole, the sector followed the government line. Unless we were at war with a country, or the Western world had decided that their behaviour was so bad that we would no longer sell our goods and services to them or there was an imminent threat to the lives of staff, there was no need for debate. But while this may be an acceptable position for purely commercial organisations, one could argue that it is not acceptable for universities. This is not an issue that only post-1992 universities have had to struggle with. All universities, from Oxford, which was criticised for accepting funding of £17.7 million from the Gulf States, to the London School of Economics (LSE), which took funding from Khadafy's son, have had questions to answer. But perhaps not enough questions have been asked.

The UK government now uses universities as economic shock troops. After all, international student fees are one of the quickest ways in which the UK can get money out of a country, especially a country that is unstable. This was seen in the case of Libya.

LIBYA

Too often the UK government has been complicit in developing an unrealistic narrative of change in countries which have dubious histories. A whiff of compromised democracy or a semi-repentant dictator, such as Libya's deposed leader Muammar Khadafy who agreed to pay billions of pounds to victims of his own terrorism, is enough for ministers to re-engage with previous pariah states. Of course, only if there is potential for profit. They also encourage British businesses to join in the opportunities that arise from decades of suppression and corruption. And since PMI, universities have been considered a business and part of the economic shock troops that the government sends in too. So when Tony Blair made friends with Libya on behalf of Shell, universities instantly forgot Lockerbie, the killing of PC Yvonne Fletcher, human rights abuses and the frankly crazy utterances of Khadafy, and joined oil companies, security firms – which of course is a euphemism for mercenaries – and arms dealers, to be the first to embrace this new market. Not surprising really, as part of the deal to end his country's pariah state, Khadafy promised to fund hundreds of thousands of students to study in the UK.

Within a year of Blair and Khadafy's agreement, a large delegation of UK higher education representatives was entertained in a beach resort near the spectacular remains of an ancient Carthaginian city. There they were given stories of how the Khadafy government was going to upgrade its higher education sector and crucially how much money it was going to spend doing it. They even took three members of the delegation out to the desert to meet the leader. Unfortunately Libya fell to bits before the universities could get much money from the regime.

When Khadafy was overthrown, with help from Britain's new prime minister Cameron, guess who turned up straight after the civil war? Yes, a trade fare complete with the exact same universities in the fore. The chaos that followed Khadafy's overthrow and the entry of ISIS into Libya meant that there was no business actually entered into. But not without trying.

SAUDI ARABIA

In Saudi Arabia homosexuals or cross-dressers face fines, floggings, life imprisonment or even death. Women until recently were not allowed to drive.

But we still line up to take the Saudi riyal. Before visa restrictions made it difficult, UK universities used to help facilitate visas for male chaperones of female students. These moral guardians were allowed to sit in the classroom keeping an eye on the young women to make sure they didn't behave like students or learn bad habits. The British Council runs a Saudi Interest Group, which is a group of more than 80 education institutions that have an interest in recruiting Saudi students and forming partnerships with Saudi institutions.

As is the case with most oil-rich Arab states, Saudi students tend to be funded by government or oil companies. These have lists of universities that they recognise, and getting on these lists is important, but also less than transparent. In 2011 at the height of the Arab Spring, the Saudi government dropped both universities in Sheffield off their list. There was little explanation given, but eventually it was admitted that there was no issue with the services of the universities, rather there were just too many Saudi students in Sheffield and the Saudi government did not want a big enough concentration of young people in one place in the UK in case they started having notions of democracy.

This could be taken as an acknowledgement that a Western education was dangerous to the Saudi regime. But the other UK universities on the list did not protest, because they were too busy hovering up the students who would have been funded to study in Sheffield.

TOOLS TO HELP MARKET CHOICE

But the truth is an argument could be made for and against working with any country that UK universities are involved with: China's one-party state and re-education of ethnic minorities, Malaysia's affirmative action, India's treatment of woman, US detainees in Guantanamo Bay and Trump.

The dilemma for universities working in countries with different ethical and moral codes is where does one decide that the differences are too much to accept. And whether by working there, are you endorsing the difference or helping change the country?

It is a can of worms, and many universities choose not to open it. Perhaps because if the ethics of working in every country was open for debate within the university' community, then there would be few countries they would engage with. And the debate would rage on forever, as there are as many reasons too as to not to.

But there are tools that could be used to help ameliorate risks and enlighten the debate. One indicator that could be used is the corruption perception index. This is a ranking of corruption in the world developed by an independent organisation, the Transparency International. They define corruption as 'the abuse of entrusted power for private gain'.

As a tool to help universities decide which countries they are more likely to have moral dilemmas working in, it is valuable. This should be used along with the ease of doing business index which is compiled yearly by the World Bank.

This shows which countries have regulatory frameworks and infrastructures that make it easier to work in. Those countries low in the index normally have high corruption rates and regulations designed to allow for the abuse of power.

One example of a market that has opened up in recent years is Myanmar. And it is a good example of how using these indexes could help universities decide on whether to engage there.

MYANMAR

On the release of Aung San Suu Kyi in 2010, after the opposition leader had spent years under house arrest, many UK universities were invited to set up partnerships and develop programmes in Myanmar.

It is not reasonable to assume that any UK university could have predicted that within a few years, Aung San Sui Kyi would be named as complicit in the crimes against Rohingya by Britain's International Development Committee, stripped of her British and Canadian honorary citizenship, the freedom of Edinburgh, the US Holocaust Museum's Elie Wiesel Award, Amnesty International would revoke its Ambassador of Conscience Award and there would be calls for her Nobel Peace Prize to be revoked. But using the corruption index and ease of doing business indexes may have helped universities understand how precarious the new democracy was and help make a decision as to whether to work in the country or not.

Since democracy, Myanmar's corruption ranking has got better. But for most of the time the index is available for (since 1995), it was the third most corrupt country in the world (Transparecy International 2019) (only bettering North Korea and Somalia). With the introduction of a sort of democracy, it jumped but only to 156th out of 177 – indicating that there was still extreme corruption endemic in the country. In 2018 it was also number 171 out of 180 in the ease of doing business index, an index that was so bad, that until 2014 it wasn't even measured.

These indexes are important, and although they would not have predicted the Rohingya crises, if used, they would have shown clearly that working in Myanmar was extremely risky. The corruption index indicates that corruption is endemic, it's built into the structure, the military control the extraction industries, and their families or clans using the profits control much more. The ease of doing business ranking is low, as regulations are designed to help the ruling elite. The majority of business people behind private higher education have links to the military or the preceding government. With so many years of such corruption, who else could have amassed the wealth needed to own a college?

And given the level of fees in comparison with the average income in the country, one could assume that the students who can afford these fees must come from the families who control the businesses.

There is of course a valid argument that unless we engage in such countries, nothing will improve. The big UK players in Myanmar are pre-1992 universities, in particular Oxford University and the OU. The universities in Myanmar were closed by the regime for many years and both the OU and Oxford are helping reopen them and train among others a new cohort of lawyers.

Both have made robust defences of their continuing presence in the country. In an article in the THES, 'Universities Pressured to Cut Myanmar Ties over Rohingya crisis', the OU stated that 'we believe that there is no more effective antidote to oppression whether it may occur than an educated population' (Bothwell 2017). The university of Oxford explained their role as 'to support peaceful and inclusive democracy, strengthening the rule of law, and the provision of greater economic opportunities through higher education' (Bothwell 2017).

The dilemma with making value judgments on whether to work in a corrupt regime is highlighted in the article in THES where Lee Jones, reader in international politics at Queen Mary University, says, 'Adequate education is one way that the racists and xenophobic attitudes and historically false beliefs driving the Rohingya crisis can be challenged and changed' (Bothwell 2017). But in the same article, Penny Green, professor of law and globalisation at the same university, says that we should be 'boycotting all government institutions in Myanmar, including higher education' (Bothwell 2017).

These views demonstrate that there is no obvious right or wrong, even in such an extreme case. So if universities decide to work in countries considered corrupt their reasoning should be transparent and be articulated clearly in any international strategy and above all should not be about profit. So it would be preferable to have a process where decisions on whether to engage in high-risk markets such as Myanmar are agreed to by some academic body rather than a commercial one.

In addition, statements about the universities' policies for dealing with government interference in programme design and delivery must be incorporated in these programmes.

If one does choose to work in countries low down the corruption index and ease of doing business rankings, there needs to be a good risk management system put in place for the safety of staff and a communication plan which includes communicating the benefits and preparing for criticism. Above all, those involved in the programme must genuinely believe that they are doing something that is designed to improve the lot of the people in the country and not about profit.

CHAPTER 11

MALAYSIA

The story of how a middle-income and relatively small Asian country became one of the biggest markets for UK universities is one of racial politics. Before Malaysian independence, the British army had fought a guerrilla war against communists in Malaysia in the so-called Malayan Emergency. Apparently it wasn't called a war, because this would affect insurance payouts to British rubber plantation owners.

With the same subtle nuances of phrasing, in 1970 the Malaysian New Economic Policy (NEP) proposed a plan to redistribute the wealth to the Malays. It was all about 'national unity', which it would achieve by 'poverty eradication' and 'the restructuring of society'. It aimed to achieve greater 'inter-ethnic economic parity'. All of which were ways of saying that there was going to be a massive injection of money and economic benefits to the Malays. All this was under the auspices of so-called 'affirmative action' (Jomo 2005).

Over the years that followed, Malays would be favoured in everything over their Chinese and Indian cousins. No matter how many generations of Chinese and Indians had been Malaysian citizens, unless they had Malay ancestors and converted to Islam they weren't entitled to the type of government patronage the bumiputeras– the people of the soil were. All businesses had to have a bumiputera as a director, all new offerings on the stock market had to be sold to bumiputera first, bumiputeras were given houses at knock-down prices. In addition to business, higher education was seen as an important part in achieving 'parity'. In the Third Malaysia Plan which followed (Malaysia Govt Press 1976), higher education was tasked with rectifying 'the existing imbalances in educational opportunities between racial and income groups' (Govt Press 1976). To do this universities had to give places to bumiputeras before non-bumis. So Chinese and Indian Malays had to attain far higher grades to enter state universities because there were very few places for them – but of course that wasn't discrimination just good political sense.

The bumiputeras were on a gravy train and the next sauce boat to come into the station was overseas university education. Malaysians were given scholarships to study overseas, which included living expenses, flights and fees. Hundreds of thousands of scholarships were awarded but only if you were Muslim and could show descent from a Malay.

At the same time, the wealthy Chinese and Indians who were being discriminated against and found it impossible to gain entrance to a Malaysian university were saving up and sending their children overseas to get a degree. This created a market for overseas education larger than one would have expected. From 1978 to 1985 the number of Malaysians studying overseas grew from 39,000 to 60,000. Around 30,000 of these studied in the UK, making Malaysia the largest non-EU market for UK universities at the time (HESA n.d.).

This number of Malaysians overseas accounted for 51.2 per cent of total higher education enrolment of Malaysians. Of this, 63 per cent were Chinese, who were self-funding whereas nearly 100 per cent of the Malay students studying overseas were funded by the government (Chai 2007).

It was a win-win situation for UK universities– take the money from the discriminated against, and at the same time take it from the discriminators.

SHEFFIELD HALLAM

One of the first private colleges in Malaysia was Tunku Abdul Rahman College (TAR). Although it was named after a Malay – the first prime minister of independent Malaysia – it was in fact a predominantly Chinese institution. It was established as a reaction to the affirmative action which discriminated against Chinese students. When it started, TAR College was not allowed to run degree-level programmes. But its three-year diploma, taught in English, was generally considered to be the equivalent of a degree and its graduates better than those from the public universities. Although they could be admitted directly into masters programmes by many UK universities, many wished to have a degree to be able to gain employment at home. Sheffield Hallam University developed a programme for these students, who were taught over the summer in the UK. Students were given credit for the three-year diploma they had completed at TAR. They came to Sheffield to study over the summer semester, and in 15 weeks the TAR students gained enough additional credit to be awarded a Sheffield Hallam degree. The time in Sheffield was sold as an all-inclusive package, including accommodation in the university, which would normally be vacant during the summer. There were also excursions and immersions in UK culture. As the accommodation was vacant anyway, and as there were thousands of students, the fees were very reasonable – in fact no other university managed to match them and steal the business. Thus a post-1992 university based in a northern industrial town helped thousands of Chinese Malays to gain a degree that their discriminatory government denied them – and made loads of dosh at the same time.

TRANSNATIONAL EDUCATION (TNE) DEVELOPMENT

When the Asian economic crisis hit, something had to be done in Malaysia about the amount of money that was being spent overseas on higher education. It was estimated that it cost about 8.5 per cent of the cumulative foreign exchange earnings of Malaysia between 1976 and 1980 to educate so many Malaysians overseas (Yilmaz 2010).

To counter this, during the Sixth Malaysian Plan (1991–95) the country adopted a policy of expanding the role of the private sector as a provider of higher education (Sixth Malaysian Plan 1991). This was part of a wider policy named Malaysia Incorporated, which had been developed to strengthen the role of the private sector in wealth creation.

The Private Higher Education Institutions Act 1996 (PHEIA) not only made the establishment of more private universities and university colleges easier but also gave financial incentives to do so. They were now allowed to teach to degree level.

This allowed them access to a new group of students. Prior to the enactment of this piece of legislation, private institutions of higher education existed, but were not authorised to teach to degree level. Instead they acted as preparatory institutions for students to undertake courses of instructions in preparation for externally conferred degrees.

As pointed out by Zuraidah Zaaba, 'The government realised that private education flourished through being able to select the medium of instruction' (Zaaba et al. 2010). The legislation specifically allowed the use of English in degree programmes taught with foreign providers, whereas the public universities taught in Malay.

This legislation opened up Malaysian private colleges for UK TNE programmes to an extent that had never been seen before. This was where UK universities and particularly post-1992 universities learned how to develop overseas programmes with private providers. In the mid-1980s there were less than 50 private higher education institutes (PHEIs). By 2000 this had become 640.

It was almost as if it was preordained. Just as post-1992 universities were beginning to look for markets, hundreds of private colleges sprung up from the rich soil of Malaysia, looking for partners who could award degrees. Partnerships made sense for the private providers; the students they were designed to attract were those that were going abroad to study. So if they could get the same degree at home, it would be significantly cheaper, and the PHEIA had been designed to encourage this trade. A separate agency, the National Accreditation Board (LAN), was set up to accredit diploma certificate and degree-level study in PHEIs and they developed accreditation procedures for foreign degrees taught in these institutes.

Australian universities were the first to transplant their degrees in these new colleges, with a few post-1992 UK universities following swiftly behind. Soon everyone wanted in on the act, even though by any standards the teaching of degrees overseas had quality risks, was less profitable than teaching the same students at home and did not contribute to internationalisation of home students. But with the Asian financial crisis hitting recruitment from South East Asia to the UK, for post-1992 universities, it was the only game in town.

As the market heated up, many post-1992 UK universities reorganised, and senior posts were created within some universities, whose sole purpose was to develop TNE programmes overseas. The measure of success of these senior staff was the number of programmes they brought back to the university to be developed and how hard they fought the 'bureaucracy' to allow for the flexibility that they required to develop them.

Both pre- and post-1992 universities were enticed to Malaysia to help with the massification of the Malaysian higher education sector. This was not part of any UK strategy but a result of commercial pressures. But while post-1992 universities took the risk of working with start-up companies, pre-1992 universities tended not to. In 2007, 85 per cent of all UK TNE in Malaysia was being carried out by post-1992 universities (HESA n.d.). By 2011, of the 32 universities offering TNE degrees in Malaysia, 23 were post-1992 universities and of the 9 pre-1992 universities, only 2 worked with private colleges, whereas 5 had their own presence in Malaysia (HESA 2013).

Perhaps this was not surprising, because many post-1992 universities had experience of running the same type of 'top-up degrees' with local UK further education (FE) colleges, where the final year was taught by lecturers in the college and had systems in place to limit risk.

But this was different; FE colleges were part of the UK state system, they were state-funded not-for-profit organisations. This was not the case in Malaysia, where the private higher education sector was mainly for profit and embraced not only genuine educators, but also property speculators and others whose business model depended on the appearance of having an education establishment to get the tax reliefs and incentives that the government granted to private colleges. Collaboration agreements were written to reflect the fact that the UK university was aware they were working with a partner whose sole aim was to make as much profit as possible and that they had put in place rigorous quality systems. Risk assessments were carried out with red, amber and green lights.

Working with organisations where one could not guarantee the motives of potential partners necessitated a change in the mindset of the people negotiating the programme and the people back home, whose role it was to maintain quality and mitigate risk. This often created tensions back in the UK, where the director of quality felt that their role was to stick rigidly to a strict interpretation of Quality Assurance Agency (QAA) guidelines, and the senior international staff felt that it was the quality department's role to ensure that they interpreted these guidelines as loosely as was necessary for them to do the deal and start the programme. There was often a pressure to work quickly, as potential partners hinted that other universities were about to sign a deal with them. Bit by bit, processes were developed such that, even if they didn't mitigate risk to the university, they at least produced a written trail which showed that it wasn't the fault of the staff involved if things went wrong.

In addition, approval had to be obtained from the Malaysian education ministry through its recently created LAN.

Eventually the programme started, invariably with far less students than promised – but they decided they may as well start as all the hard work had been done.

Through trial and error, numbers built up, quality systems were embedded and money was made. According to the Eight Malaysia Plan, by the end of 2000 'private institutions provided a total of 32,480 places at degree level, 116,265 at diploma level and 60,840 at certificate level compared to 15,000 students in private higher education in 1985' (Chai 2007).

The relative success of working in this environment in Malaysia shaped how post-1992 universities approached TNE in other countries. Many private colleges and partnerships failed. But there were also significant success stories. There were many cases where UK universities started working with a partner at the start of their journey from a shop lot college with a few hundred students housed above a hairdresser's, to a university college with thousands of students in a landscaped campus that looked just like architects' drawings. It was to these success stories that senior staff, tasked with expanding TNE throughout the world, looked to whenever they were questioned about doing business with partners that had no premises, no staff and only good connections to the local ministry of education. By 2007 there were 21,000 students studying UK degrees in Malaysia this had risen to 58,000 by 2010 and held steady at that rate. However, this hid an underlying statistic – the number of students studying post-1992 universities began to decline as the numbers in pre-1992 universities increased.

MALAYSIA AS AN EDUCATION HUB

The Malaysian government had ambitions to attract international students. In 2002 Singapore announced its global schoolhouse concept with a target of attracting 150,000 international students by 2015. Soon after, Malaysia announced its intention of becoming a regional hub for international students with 100,000 by 2010.

The only way for this to be possible was through private higher education. After all, the public universities were full to bursting, mainly taught in Malaya, and did not have a good reputation, with none in the top rankings.

The Malaysian government followed the UK and Australian model and opened promotion offices in Beijing, Jakarta, Dubai and Ho Chi Ming City. These promoted Malaysia as a cheap, safe and friendly Muslim nation. With programmes from 'top' Western universities, private providers were encouraged to use the promotions offices to attract students, and recruitment fairs surprisingly similar to the UK ones were held throughout the world. It was a success, and in 2005, Malaysia had 50,380 foreign students, mainly from East Asia and the Pacific region, of whom about 82 per cent were in private HEIs (Chai 2007). So no surprise that the politicians had announced a new target of 200,000 by 2020.

By 2015 there was 151,979 international students studying in the country, of which 80.3 per cent were in private institutes. Of this, some 131,000 were in higher education (*New Straits Times* 2016). UNESCO ranked Malaysia 12th in its top 20 countries for international students in 2014 (British Council 2016).

INTERNATIONALISATION OF MALAYSIA HIGHER EDUCATION

The attraction of foreign universities to award their degrees in Malaysia in some ways meant that many Malaysians were gaining an international education at home. A report on the impact of TNE on host countries commissioned by the

British Council conducted a survey of 8 stakeholder types over 10 countries including Malaysia, concluded:

> The importance of increased awareness and knowledge about international issues and events has been clearly understood by TNE students, as they believe that TNE can help them gain this international understanding. There is corroborating evidence that this rationale and expectation is met for TNE students. When asked which skills had been enhanced by TNE, international outlook ranked second in importance after analytical skills. (Going Global 2014)

Whether this 'international outlook' actually means a Western outlook, however, is unclear in the research. At the same time that Malaysian students received a Western education, UK universities adapted their programmes to suit the Malaysian environment. Most UK universities, teaching with partners in Malaysia have three intakes a year and run concentrated programmes so students work over the summer semester and get a degree in two years rather than three at home at a cheaper price.

This has not been transferred to home campuses. Presumably there is some academic argument that prevents it happening at home, or it could be that universities are wary of receiving less students and fees if they have a concentrated degree at home.

TNE also helped internationalisation of Malaysian Higher education by helping in the recruitment of international students to Malaysia. The majority came to private providers. Thus the private college students were getting Western qualifications taught in English in classrooms where the student body was increasingly international. This was not the case for public universities. Apart from those teaching some specialist subjects such as Islamic banking and Islamic law, the majority had few international students, and employers felt that their students were not as well equipped to work in the private sector as graduates from TNE programmes (Zaaba et al. 2010).

As the private education sector in Malaysia matured, the private colleges were allowed to become universities in their own right and award their own degrees, so they reduced or divested themselves of the assistance that post-1992 universities had given them. The Malaysian government concentrated in attracting 'top' universities to develop campuses to help with their ambitions to attract good quality international students

This has pushed some foreign TNE providers, who are not considered by the MOE to be the quality to be allowed to open a campus, to review whether to continue TNE or not, but in most cases encouraged them to look for new developing markets.

The story of UK universities in Malaysia is still evolving, but leaves some questions. Not least as to whether it should be the role of UK universities to assist other countries to internationalise and improve their education system while gaining few benefits other than short-term financial rewards.

Despite the rhetoric of developing win-win sustainable partnerships, most UK universities' TNE starts out with a view that the UK university is the senior partner and the overseas partner less developed, hence their desire to pay for the UK qualification. However as countries' higher education systems develop, it is clear that this dynamic changes and if there has been little investment by the UK partner they become surplus to requirement.

By running TNE programmes, in the short-term, post-1992 universities were able to continue to earn some income from Malaysian students who had been hit by the Asian economic crisis and were less able to afford to study in the UK. But as the private sector matured in Malaysia, its government strategy was to phase out what it considered to be lower-level foreign universities. At the same time the Malaysian government gave financial incentives for those universities which it considered to be more prestigious to open campuses in country, none of which are post-1992. These became at the forefront of the Malaysian government's international recruitment strategy. Thus by developing a strategy for internationalisation and relying on Western universities' greed, the Malaysian government has developed a higher education sector which is international in content and student body. Post-1992 universities having developed substantial TNE presence in Malaysia are finding that the returns are diminishing. By concentrating on financial rewards, they have failed to develop sustainable business. However, pre-1992 universities who have campuses in Malaysia should take cognisance of the fate of their post-1992 colleagues. The government of Malaysia could at some time in the future decide that it no longer needs their presence.

CHAPTER 12

CHINA

EXPANSION OF CHINESE HIGHER EDUCATION SYSTEM

Education has been highly valued in China since the time of Confucius and the civil servants exams, which could be taken by clever people of any social class. For centuries the way to become a Mandarin, a civil servant, who would control vast swathes of the country was by excelling in the formal exam system. And education is still seen as the way to success. Students in primary schools study long hours to get to a good secondary school and then study even longer for the Gaokao – the national university entrance exam – to gain entry to a prestigious university. Those with money employ Gaokao nannies, attend boot camps or top scorer hotels, all feel the stress of expectations. A low score almost guarantees a lifetime of low-ranking jobs and family disappointment. With the one-child policy – which has recently been relaxed – each child sitting the exam has two parents and four grandparents relying on them solely for the families status.

The ministry of education (MOE) has, what is in effect, a league of Tier 1 and Tier 2 universities and Tier 1 and Tier 2 students. It is not a league table in the same way that the world rankings work where they look at various metrics to judge the relative position of each university. Rather the MOE decides which universities it chooses to be the best and diverts funding, staff and students to these. Extra funding is given to those universities who they decide are top of the rankings and the top universities are able to choose the best students from the national exam, although there are some anomalies in quotas for students in cities rather than in the country. So in China it's no surprise that Chinese students and academics are obsessed with league tables. In their country there is no dubiety as to which is the best university and the hardest to get into as this is decided at the top level by the state.

In the late 1990s, it was not only the UK that was looking to expand higher education. However, whereas the UK had begun that expansion through the polytechnics from the 1980s and continued it through the 1990s, China was well behind.

Until the late 1990s participation in higher education had stayed at around 7 per cent. In 1996 the 9th Five-Year Plan encouraged development through science and technology rather than cheap labour and exports of resources. The plan said that China should 'implement the strategy of revitalising the nation by relying on science and education and help forge close ties between science, technology, education and economy' (CPC Central Committee 1995).

The 9th Five Year Plan recognised that a factor that would impede economic progress in the medium to long term was 'pressures in matching the economic scientific and technological superiority of the developed countries in the increasingly stiff international competition'.

It was clear that a major driver to revitalise the nation and make it competitive in the medium to long term must be an improved higher education sector and there was increasing pressure from an exam-obsessed population to have more places available for all.

In 1998 China enacted a law to redevelop the higher education system in 'the service of the socialist modernization drive' (MOE 1998). The MOE needed to massively increase its higher education sector and ensure it was fit for its concept of centrally managed capitalism In 1998 they were behind most Asian countries in terms of participation, and they wanted to compete on the world stage not just Asia.

Since Confucius, the Chinese idea of education was to produce graduates able to work in the civil services and use what they were taught for the good of society. Since then, this has changed little; the role of higher education was clear in the 1998 law, there was no argument about education for education's sake. It said, 'Educatees shall become builders and successors for the socialist cause [...] The task of higher education is to train people to become senior specialists imbued with the spirit of creativeness and the ability of practice, to develop science, technology and culture and to promote the socialist modernization drive' (MOE 1998).

From 1998 there was an expansion, which could equate to the speed of the expansion of the railways 20 years later. From 1998 the enrolment of new regular undergraduate students on average grew by about 26.9 per cent annually. As a result, the total enrolment of regular undergraduate students in Chinese higher education increased from 3.41 million in 1998 to 13.33 million in 2004 to 37 million by 2016. In 1998 there was a 6.4 per cent participation rate, by 2016 this was 42.7 per cent.

DIGESTING HIGHER EDUCATION

But while expanding the MOE decided that they must look to other successful higher education systems and learn from them. They did not want to create a system that was insular. They wanted to have an internationalised modern higher education system that could compete with the best in the world. They recognised that in technology and science the developed nations were ahead.

Internationalisation was managed by the MOE, as the Chinese did later with the railways. They went about taking the best bits of other systems, changing them to suit themselves, using this new hybrid education to modernise their own system and then competing with the universities who they had paid to help them internationalise – in effect digesting education.

The first thing they did was to learn about other education systems, including the UK, for themselves. First was a visit to Britain from a potential partner. It could take quite some time to organise, because travel outside China was restricted for senior government officials and all sorts of invitation letters had to be sent.

There they were told that the UK higher education system created more creative entrepreneurial graduates, just what the Chinese government was encouraging their higher education system to do. But no one in a British university stopped to suggest that Asia had the most entrepreneurs in the current age.

But even if one agrees that a Western education does develop creativity, it does so by emphasising the individual. To the Chinese the individual is important but only within a societal context. Chinese tradition focuses on the individual as a vitally integrated element within a larger familial, social, political and cosmic whole not as someone whose main responsibility is to self-fulfillment.

Thus, in a system where the university Communist Party secretary can outrank the president, and the party considers its strength to be as a collective, the notion that the focus of higher education was to develop individualism was alien and definitely not the way to create a Chinese version of higher education.

In the end the principals of Chinese universities and top staff in the MOE realised there were limitations in their higher education system but also recognised that there were strengths.

They decided that they wanted to keep their competitive Confucian style of education but add a Western flavour – just enough to give graduates the tools to be entrepreneurial and creative, improve their English and give them the international experience that was increasingly needed in Chinese businesses but without encouraging too much individualism. This was the Chinese way of internationalisation and was carried out through digesting Western higher education in a number of different levels; syllabus design, research and staff training.

The extent of their success would be measured by league tables.

SYLLABUS DESIGN/JOINT PROGRAMMES

UK universities working in China developed articulation arrangements with Chinese universities where students from partners would come to the UK for the final year of a degree after studying the Chinese degree for three years (Chinese undergraduate degrees are of four-year duration). If they successfully passed the final year in the UK they were awarded a UK degree.

These arrangements were not binding and so students in many Chinese partner universities had a choice of UK universities or other countries to go to if another university pitched up and signed their own articulation agreement.

The Chinese MOE was aware of these arrangements and wanted to ensure that the Chinese universities were getting something out of the relationships rather than it just being a form of recruitment for foreign universities and benefiting a small number of students who could afford to study in the UK. So they developed new regulations to ensure that China would benefit.

COOPERATION OF FOREIGN SCHOOLS REGULATIONS

In 2003, regulations were published to regulate cooperation with foreign schools and make sure that foreign universities were contributing to China's view of internationalisation (MOE 2003). The regulations stated that foreign universities could only teach in China with a Chinese partner. They encouraged local universities to develop joint degrees with foreign partners by giving them larger quotas and allowing them to charge a student premium. These regulations were developed to ensure that all Chinese students in a joint degree would have the chance to have some international experience. The plan was also to have some internationalisation of Chinese academic staff as well.

Foreign universities including UK ones realised that China was the fastest growing market in the world and jumped at the chance of MOE-approved programmes where numbers would be more or less guaranteed even if it meant that they would be operating under MOE rules, which were not quite compatible with the UK quality systems. What resulted was a game of cat and mouse where the MOE changed regulations to ensure that the foreign universities were running programmes that would contribute to their strategic internationalisation aims, whereas the Quality Assurance Agency (QAA) documented how UK universities ignored their guidelines or tailored their models to take advantage of them.

BALANCING MOE REGULATIONS AND QAA GUIDELINES

In China, from the publishing of the regulations for cooperation with foreign schools in 2003, there was an explosion of what the Chinese side termed joint degrees. At around the same time, the QAA brought out a revised version of the collaborative provision section of its code, which had guidelines for joint, dual and double awards.

The QAA guidelines were not helpful for universities who wished to apply to the MOE for a joint programme. To conform to them they would have to have oversight of the Chinese universities teaching and examinations. So, UK universities decided to claim to the MOE that they were running joint degrees. But at home they described them as articulations that were no different from the previous model.

For Chinese students to gain what the MOE called a joint degree, they would have to come to the UK for the final year of the UK degree. If they were successful, the Chinese partner gave credit and awarded their degree when the students returned.

But as far as the MOE was concerned, all students on these approved programmes had enrolled on a joint degree in China and should have the opportunity to gain a dual award and have a third of the teaching done by the Western partner. In this model, only those that came to the UK actually gained a joint degree and had the amount of input from the UK partner that the MOE required.

NEW THINKING BY MOE

The MOE felt that foreign universities were not delivering what they expected and were aware that UK universities were calling these programmes articulations and trying to minimise the input in China that they had to deliver. In effect they were recruitment devices. The MOE wanted to push the foreign universities into real partnerships with Chinese universities.

By 2011 the Chinese government was voicing concerns about whether these joint programmes were delivering the international education that they wished. This had followed a round of approvals in 2011 where the MOE had rejected 70 per cent of applications. They put a temporary freeze on all new approvals, although it being China, some still squeaked through approvals.

A number of provinces were asked to evaluate the existing joint programmes in their province. The results of these pilot evaluations were never published; in 2012 the MOE announced a nation-wide evaluation of all approved joint programmes. The purpose of these evaluations was to bring joint programmes in line with China's needs rather than a foreign partner's wish list. On 22 January 2012, the following was reported in an article in University World News: 'China to evaluate foreign university presence and prepare guidelines' (Sharma 2012).

> Beijing-based diplomats, speaking on condition of anonymity, said the government was seeking to align new foreign provision more closely with China's national interests as it moves towards a knowledge economy under its 2010–20 'innovation society' plan. (Sharma 2012)

As a result of this evaluation, in 2014 the MOE tightened the approval process as they felt that many collaborations were not conforming to their regulations, which among other things stated that the foreign partner had to provide one-third of the teaching input. Over two hundred approvals were rescinded and a new stricter approval process was put in place.

In a speech at the Sino Australia Forum on transnational education in March 2015, Yao Bingchen, the head of MOE stated:

> China encourages the Chinese universities and foreign universities to exploit more cooperation opportunities in agriculture, forestry, medical science, engineering and leading-edge inter-disciplinary areas that are in dire need. This adjustment suits the present economic development of China. It is fair to say that we have trained enough talents specialized in business or commercial management.

He went on to say:

> We require systematic introduction of high-quality educational resources from foreign universities and Chinese-foreign double certificates in China so that students can get access to overseas study without going abroad. (Bingchen 2015)

This clearly pointed the direction that the MOE wished future collaborations to take. New programmes should give the students the chance to gain the foreign degree in China as well as being given the opportunity to study abroad. This effectively blew a hole in the previous business model, which relied on students studying in the UK and the UK universities having minimal resources in China.

Since the speech, UK universities were encouraged to not only have joint programmes but also set up joint colleges with partners. These run a suite of joint programmes but have a physical entity which is considered to be a faculty or school of the Chinese university. Although they are joint entities, the Chinese partner appoints the most senior member of staff and has more members on the management committee than the foreign partner. The reason the Chinese government has been keen for these to be developed is that they necessitate a year-round presence from the foreign university although many foreign universities are trying to limit this to as few members of staff as possible. One rule is that the foreign university has not to make a profit from these joint colleges. But with a bit of creative accounting around real costs, this can be disguised.

DODGY COLLEGES DOING BUSINESS IN CHINA

China sits at 87 out of 180 in the world corruption perception rankings. Working in the country has its challenges. Since the late 1990s when more and more universities in the UK engaged with China, the onus has always been to understand and embrace the differences in cultures albeit in a superficial way.

There were numerous disasters mostly due to a lack of fundamental understanding of working in China.

Higher education in China appears to be well regulated and under far more central control then in the UK. However, the rule of law is far less strong in China than in the UK. The Chinese have a saying, 'The Emperor is all powerful, but the Emperor is over the mountains and far away.'

A small number of UK universities found that after a visit from a senior member of staff, the Chinese partner had gone ahead and gained approval from the relevant authorities to open a joint college. The UK partners had merely signed a general memorandum of understanding saying they would like to work together.

In 2014, the MOE substantially improved its processes and in 2014 closed down 200 joint programmes and 5 joint ventures which had either never started or the foreign partner had never heard of it. Now as part of the approval process, UK universities are asked if they know about the application.

Even without partners who are breaking the rules, there are fundamental differences in approach, which can rear its confusing head. The idea that once a contract is signed, the negotiations are finished is a Western one. For the Chinese, the contract is merely a framework around which there can be continuous negotiations. Academic staff arrive in China to develop the next stage of a business studies degree only to find the partner asking if they could run a media studies degree instead, or if they could run the UK final year in China, which had been discussed long and hard and it had been agreed this would not happen.

There is also often a belief that in a rigid hierarchy like Chinese universities there is no place for office politics. That is far from the truth; UK universities often find themselves in the middle of battles between international colleges of the university and the faculties. But they are unaware of this; all they know is that they had agreed to run a programme, sent the contract out to be signed and then never heard anything again.

SCOTTISH QUALIFICATIONS AUTHORITY (SQA)

It wasn't just UK universities that were working in Chinese higher education. As part of the devolved Scottish administration's push to have more income from international education activities and its stated objective in its 'Strategy for a Wider Engagement in China to expand the awarding of Scottish Awards in China' (Scottish Government 2006), the Scottish Qualifications Authority (SQA) was encouraged to work in China.

The Scottish government saw this as a way to not only make income in China but also to provide a pipeline of students into advanced levels of degrees in Scotland. At the same time, the Chinese government was looking to develop foundation programmes that would allow middle-income students who had failed to gain entry to a Chinese university the chance to get an international education experience and increase the number and breadth of vocational diplomas in China.

To this effect, the Chinese government signed agreements with IDP Australia, the Canadian International Management Institute and the SQA.

The SQA partnered with the Chinese Service Centre for Scholarly Exchange (CSCSE), an affiliated body of the MOE, whose role is to engage in educational services and support international exchanges. The role of CSCSE was to introduce partners to the SQA that carried out its own evaluation of whether these partners were capable of teaching the SQA higher national diploma (HND).

Amazingly, given that the HND is assessed and taught in English and is a significantly different educational experience than any diploma taught in China, in a matter of a few months, or indeed weeks, the SQA approved 16 institutions. By doing so they claimed that they had the resources and staff, with relevant experience needed to teach their diplomas. This showed a speed of working unprecedented in an organisation that only three months before had sent out the wrong exam marks to 6,000 students and, despite government enquiries, had taken three months to send the correct ones out.

A memorandum of understanding (MOU) was signed in November 2003 and students were enrolled in the first HND modules in September 2004. But to enrol in the HND one had to do a one-year foundation first, so the first students must have been enrolled in the foundation only weeks after the MOU was signed. The first graduates graduated with the HND in 2006 although by then there were only eight centres still approved as eight had been taken off the list.

One may question whether the speed of these approvals shows that money was more important than quality, but of course the SQA is a UK awarding body. They make the regulations for their own qualifications and so decide the quality of the final product.

It may be that in fact CSCSE had supplied the SQA with such top-quality partners that they sailed through the approvals process. On the face of it that may have been true. In all the literature and press statements the SQA released about their work in China, they claimed to be working with universities. This can be seen from the following quotes from a response to questions in the Scottish parliament about their work in China in 2007 (Scottish Government 2017):

> The first cohort of SQA HND candidates graduated from SQA-approved universities in China in June 2006.
>
> The first 3 years of the programme are delivered in Chinese universities.
>
> The table shows the number of Chinese universities approved as SQA centres doubled after the first year.

And if one looks at their website, they claim to have partnered with some top universities including Renmin University in Beijing – the Oxford or Cambridge of China.

However, if one looks closer, it is not Renmin that run the programmes but a college affiliated to the university, which was the case with almost all the initial partners.

While the agreement brokered through CSCSE was with the universities which have quality resources, the actual programme was farmed out to colleges, many of them private entities over which the university had little or no control.

In 2005 there were press reports about lecturers in one of the institutions, the Sea Rich Sino-British College, being beaten up because they uncovered 'widespread fraud involving courses run by the Scottish Qualifications Authority (SQA). Students, who paid £1,150, were promised a Higher National Diploma (HND) by local staff whether they passed the exams or not. The students were told that the qualification would guarantee them a job in Britain' (Fracassini 2005).

An interesting fact about this was that the abuse was reported to the chairman of the SQA by the part owner of the college, a Canadian businessman. He claimed that the SQA had been slow to react until he went public with his concerns. While this may well have been an isolated incident and the SQA suspended the college, it shows the truth of the SQA's work in China. They were working with private colleges not universities. Sea Rich was owned by a shipping company, other colleges are owned by property companies but affiliated to a university.

But a more telling issue, was the attempt to influence Scottish universities entrance policies. This was because the model they had agreed with the CSCSE was a four-year undergraduate degree or a five-year masters degree with the first three being up to HND in China. In Scotland this would necessitate entrance to final year of the honours degree after passing the three years in China.

So, when the 16 colleges in China were approved, the SQA asked all Scottish universities if they would allow students who had completed the HND in China access into final year (fourth year) of their degrees. As they had already come to an agreement with 34 English universities who would allow Chinese HND students into their final year (third year).

In effect, they were asking Scottish universities to allow fee-paying Chinese HND students into final year, that is, year four, when they would only accept Scottish students with the exact same qualifications into year three. They were specifically targeting post-1992 universities who were the main route into university-level programmes from HNDs in Scotland.

However, every one of them realised the potential disaster that would occur if they agreed to the SQAs request and refused.

Despite the obvious risk to the SQA's reputation in Scotland, they still persisted. In a submission to the Scottish parliament in 2008, they mention that CSCSE were keen to encourage more students to study in Scotland but not into third year. As SQA says in the submission: 'They (CSCSE) also welcome any proposals from Scottish HEIs for flexible approaches to achieving the full credits necessary for an Honours/Masters degree. SQA continues to be willing to act as a broker for discussions around this area' (SQA 2008).

This idea of being a mere broker seems strange as surely any discussion as to level of award and credit would be between the awarding body and the universities.

The students' final award in China was an SQA HND and this would be the entry qualification, so it is difficult to see what brokering the SQA needed to do between the CSCSE and Scottish universities.

A cynical person may believe that this was a way of making sure that should Scottish universities take the bait and accept the fee-paying Chinese students at a higher level than non-fee-paying home students with the same qualification, and should the press find out about it, the SQA could claim to have been merely a broker.

Despite more 'brokering' encouraged by the Scottish government, no Scottish university accepted these students into final year.

However, there are several thousand such students who study final year in English universities. In the SQA China website there are 29 UK partner universities listed that take these students into year three. All 29 are post-1992 English universities.

SORTING IT OUT

When the problems with Sea Rich College was outed in the press, the SQA took steps to manage their China expansion in a more realistic manner. There was an internal investigation, which was never published, and a number of colleges were dropped and there was a so-called reorganisation of the staff involved.

Material was developed to train Chinese staff and a more hands-on approach taken. Currently the SQA runs programmes in 34 centres, which they still claim to be universities. While some are still private colleges affiliated with Chinese universities, many are schools or departments of universities, although many of these are separate legal entities.

The story of the SQA in China is not unique. They realised that to work in China requires a different skill set. It is essential to respond quickly and be as flexible as possible. But it is also important to maintain your integrity, especially if your reputation is at risk. As the SQA found out, it is a hard balance to strike for a public organisation which has been forced into commercial ventures overseas.

INTERNATIONALISATION

As we can see, over the last 20 years there has developed a Chinese version of internationalisation. The Chinese government has a view of what they need from graduates in the future and has developed strategies to create qualifications that fit their purpose. They have used financial incentives to attract a range of universities to assist them to develop an education system that takes elements of Western higher education and marries it with Chinese. This is planned, managed and funded. If education is a market and we are all in competition as the UK government would have us believe, then perhaps we have been selling our intellectual property to China cheaply. Teaching at undergraduate level has digested elements of Western teaching, research has become more collaborative, staff and students are more aware of educational practices elsewhere and there is the beginning of a more international student body.

But the West does not see this as an example of best practice in internationalisation.

As far as commentators are concerned, the Chinese higher education system is outdated and is dismissed for being only about rote memory and competitive examinations.

According to UK educationalists, our system develops creative graduates and theirs doesn't. No questions that when countries such as the UK really had been a tangibly measurable creative power – the real world leader in engineering and technology – universities were more like their modern-day Asian counterparts than they are now. The current 'student-centred' approach in the UK and other main English-speaking destinations (MESD) countries was developed in response to massification of higher education rather than a fundamental belief in an approach that has less contact hours. UK universities have adapted their own modules to have more contact time in order to fulfil the MOE requirements.

Internationalisation is not about homogeneous systems where one could be studying in any country. It is important to have one's own culture and values and to understand and empathise with others. And where education is a tradable service, it's important to be competitive.

The method that internationalisation is planned and integrated into existing systems in China is different from the unplanned bottom-up internationalisation, which is a feature of Western higher education. Yes, there are government initiatives such as PMI that encourage universities to become involved in international activities. But the reality of the UK government international strategies from PMI to this day is that they are not in fact strategies, they are statements of intent. They always consist of a figure of international students they want to achieve (most recently including TNE) but do not consist of a plan to achieve this. That can be seen by the attempts of PMI2 to get universities to enter new markets – PMI2 had a statement that the government wanted to increase the number of countries that sent over 10,000 students a year to the UK but no plan as to how to do it and no way of persuading the universities to prioritise the markets they identified. It was left to the bottom (i.e. universities) to make the strategic decisions as to the markets they prioritised.

The fact that the Chinese see individualism differently should not be dismissed but something that one can learn from. Our programmes promote individual ambition, but perhaps it is time to develop the same understanding of Asian collective responsibility. After all, China will be the biggest economy in the world soon and we will have to work with and for them.

CHAPTER 13

AMERICA

To many Americans, America is the world.

Teams from American baseball leagues compete for world championships in a sport that no one else plays. In a wimpy version of rugby, overpadded and overweight players throw a ball around and call it football, while calling actual football, played by billions, soccer.

They put the date the wrong way around, despise the metric system and can't understand why the rest of the world thinks that being allowed to carry guns is not a fundamental human right.

American films show buses driving around London with the legend 'London, England', or pictures of the Eiffel tower as 'Paris, France', presumably to differentiate them from those well-known world centres such as London Ohio or Paris Texas.

But what can you expect from a country where until the early 1990s less than 10 per cent of the population held passports?

When the Iron Curtain was firmly drawn shut and China was cut off from the rest of the world, there wasn't much chance to learn about the competition. And as for the rest, why bother?

But all that changed with the end of the Cold War, the opening up of China, and terrorism being brought to the heart of America on 9/11.

These were the fundamental drivers towards the increased interest in internationalisation of higher education shown by the US government. Whereas, as shown in previous chapters, the UK government's main driver for internationalisation was commercial interest, and China's was to be able to compete with the West and still maintain its unique culture, the US government's main driver is all about national security, and it certainly isn't about fee income.

THE US GOVERNMENT'S INTERNATIONALISATION FOR NATIONAL SECURITY

The UK, through government initiatives which started with PMI, and continued up to an international education strategy in 2019, concentrated on encouraging commercial exploitation of universities and selling the UK higher education system (Dept. of Education, Dept. of International Trade 2019). As seen in preceding chapters, at the government level in the UK, there have been some muted attempts to increase study-abroad opportunities for British students. But they mainly consisted of limited funding for scholarships and more advertising of opportunities.

In America there have been a variety of government-level initiatives, which were more ambitious, although doomed to fail.

In the early 1990s, the David Borden National Security Education Act was passed. In the introduction of the legislation, it states quite clearly the objectives for increasing internationalisation of higher education: 'The future national security and economic well-being of the United States will depend substantially on the ability of its citizens to communicate and compete by knowing the languages and cultures of other countries' (Borden 1991).

In a country where at the time only 7 per cent of the population had passports (Hyde 2004), this was a major challenge and worry. A fund, the National Security Education Trust Fund (NSET), was established, which was intended to manage a scheme of scholarships and grants that would be awarded to students who wanted to study abroad in countries designated as 'of importance to the national security interests of the United States, and are, therefore, critical countries' (Borden 1991). There was also money made available to universities to teach languages deemed to be 'critical'; those students who were awarded scholarships had to sign up to work for the federal government after graduation.

GLOBAL COMPETENCIES AND NATIONAL NEEDS

In 2005, a report by the Abraham Lincoln Commission on Study Abroad entitled 'Global Competencies and National Needs' (GCNN) was published (Abraham Lincoln Commission on Study Abroad 2005).

The commission wanted to massify and democratise study abroad. It would have made a radical change not only to American students but also to American society though not necessarily in the way that educators would have welcomed.

It proposed that by 2016, 50 per cent of all higher education graduates would have some form of learning experience overseas. Quite a contrast to the UK government's study abroad goal in 2018 of having 13 per cent of UK students having some study abroad as part of their undergraduate degree.

Not only were there to be one million American students studying abroad annually by 2016 but also study abroad was to be 'democratised'. The aim was for study-abroad students to have the same demographic mix as was present in the overall system. Given that over 40 per cent of students in American higher education are at community colleges which have little experience with overseas study and the students are generally from poor backgrounds, this would be a major undertaking and would require funding of an unprecedented level.

It was estimated that the fellowships would cost $50 million at start up, rising to a steady state of $125 million per year.

The findings of the commission resulted in the Abraham Lincoln Study Abroad Act of 2006, and then in March 2007, the Senator Paul Simon Study Abroad Foundation Act was passed by both houses.

Whether it was written to gain support from all parties or not, the report is a snapshot of the US government's views of internationalisation – not so much about how to do it, but why it is necessary. Reading it now, we can see the view of America that Trump and his anti-globalisation followers used to gain power.

'To protect our borders, and defend our interest abroad' would seem like the mission for an international police agency. But in fact, it is the reason given by the commission to dramatically increase the numbers of American students studying abroad. The rhetoric of national security to encourage investment in study abroad had been used before by Borden and others. The commission report, GCNN, quotes from a report compiled in 2004 by the two major bodies that promote study abroad – NAFSA Association for International Educators and Alliance for International Education and Cultural Exchange they argued for more funding of study abroad – thus: 'We no longer have the option of getting along without the expertise that we need to understand and conduct our relations with the world. We do not have the option of not knowing our enemies' (Abraham Lincoln Commission on Study Abroad 2005).

GCNN goes on to 'remember the desperate search for speakers of Arabic, Farsi, and Pashto that followed the national calamity of September 11, 2001. A more dramatic demonstration of the importance of study abroad would be difficult to find' (Abraham Lincoln Commission on Study Abroad 2005).

Even though the Lincoln scholarship was never funded, the report and the legislation that followed showed an alarming insight into the US government's view of the drivers for internationalisation through study abroad.

But in America, at a government level, internationalisation of higher education has been unsuccessful. Despite cross-party support and impressive targets, funding has not followed.

ON-CAMPUS STUDENTS AS A THREAT TO NATIONAL SECURITY

Given the view that American students could be used to help fight against a host country, it is no surprise that recently the federal government has worried that, as hosts to the largest number of foreign students in the world, they are sowing the seeds of their own destruction.

The ongoing trade war with China and fears about China's attitude towards IP has meant that the 350,000 Chinese students in America have begun to be viewed as a potential national security threat. In a report in the *Financial Times* it was claimed that the White House discussed a total ban on Chinese students. According to the article, 'In February, Christopher Wray, director of the FBI, said his agency was increasingly worried about China's use of "non-traditional" intelligence collectors, including students, professors and scientists' (Sevastopulo 2018). He also indicated that 'other countries are seeking to use academics and researchers to steal cutting-edge research and technology' (O'Malley 2018). However, it was China that the FBI was most worried about, according to Wray who claimed that 'no country poses a broader, more severe intelligence collection threat than China' (O'Malley 2018). This has been followed by similar worries from the British MI5 and Australian security authorities.

The plan to ban all Chinese students from America was shelved when Terry Branstad, the governor of Iowa and former ambassador to China, highlighted the economic impact and observed that it would affect small colleges more than the more prestigious ones.

This is part of an increasingly widespread view in American circles of the American university system being used and manipulated for Chinese and other foreign governments' purposes. After all, that's what they would do if they could get the funding.

REALITY OF STUDY ABROAD

Thankfully, in practice, because of a lack of government funding, study abroad in America has not been part of a top-down strategy, but has been led by individuals and individual institutions.

While the US government sees study abroad as a matter of national security, for colleges and students this is not the main driver.

This is plainly illustrated in the countries students choose to study in. In 2016/17 there were over 300,000 outbound American students (IIE 2018). The top destination is the UK, with the top five destinations, which account for 40 per cent of all study abroad, being European. I doubt that even the Trump administration believes that Britain and Italy constitute a threat to national security.

AMERICA'S ATTITUDE TOWARD AGENTS

American universities successfully recruit international students but they do so in a manner that is significantly different to their UK and Australian competitors. As shown in previous chapters, the aggressive and sometimes morally dubious aspects of UK universities' recruitment has been as a result of chronic underfunding. American universities may complain about underfunding but they are massively better funded than any other country's higher education sector apart from Luxembourg (OECD 2017).

The UK government's strategies have concentrated on the economic benefits of international recruitment. This not only justified but also encouraged UK universities' aggressive international recruitment tactics.

But the US government's strategies have hardly mentioned direct economic benefits of international on-campus students, concentrating mainly on national security and soft power. And crucially, at both state and federal government level, there has been active discouragement of commercial-style recruitment tactics.

In particular, the US government's view of the inappropriateness of the use of recruitment agents developed an argument around the morals of international recruitment that was completely bypassed in the UK. The tenor of this argument, in America, has meant that seeing international students as cash cows is not an acceptable view of the purpose of international recruitment. And thus, the extreme commercialisation of international recruitment which characterises those UK universities low in the league tables has not been duplicated by the Americans in the main.

America's, anti-recruitment-agents stance has come about due to historical differences in the systems, particularly around funding. The introduction of significant fees for home students has been a new phenomenon in the UK, which has only recently brought about a new level of debate around admission processes and a new regulatory body – the office for students.

But in America, fees have been a fact of life for generations of US citizens. Saving towards your child's college fees is presented as noble and the American thing to do whatever your economic background.

The idea that middlemen could profit from this has always been seen as unacceptable. Therefore, in the United States, it is illegal to use commission-based agents to recruit domestic students. This was reiterated in 2011 by the U.S. Department of Education's Office of Postsecondary Education in their Program Integrity Regulations, which addressed the issue of 'incentive compensation and misrepresentation' (Secretary for Education 2011).

So, in America, given that it was felt that it was unethical to recruit domestic students through agents, it was hard to argue that it was okay to use them for international students. Philip Altbach, a prominent educational researcher who writes on internationalisation of higher education, wrote in 2011 in the University World News: 'Agents and recruiters are impairing academic standards and integrity and should be eliminated or severely curtailed. Providing information to prospective students is fine, but money should not change hands during the admissions process, and universities should not hand the power to admit – after all, a key academic responsibility – to agents or entities overseas'. As he went on to write, agents are

> not information providers, the agents are sales people. Their purpose is to sell a product, and they can use any required methods [...] abolish them. Agents and recruiters have no legitimate role in international higher education. They are unnecessary and often less than honest practitioners who stand in the way of a good flow of information to prospective students and required data about these students to academic institutions in the host countries. (Altbach 2011)

This level of feeling against recruitment agents is alien in the UK where the discussion has always been about how to use agents effectively and safely rather than whether it is acceptable to use them at all.

Before variable fees were introduced in the UK, there had never been any incentive for UK universities to use agents for domestic students.

So in the late 1990s when UK universities were approached by agents to recruit international students, there was no government or sector-wide perceived wisdom regarding their use. The idea was completely novel.

Individual universities made their own decisions, which inevitably, due to economics, led to almost every university in the UK employing agents somewhere in the world. The government, through the British Council, did not discourage this and in some ways helped the spread by developing voluntary codes of practice and agent training. These were designed to give the appearance of a regulated sector, while allowing universities the freedom to ignore the code of practice, as and when they wished.

Although funding is not as pressing an issue for American universities as it has been in the UK, since the turn of the century and the economic crisis, there has been increasing commercial need for American universities to recruit internationally. Therefore, more and more American universities entered the market and many found that to successfully recruit in major markets such as India and China required the use of agents and signed contracts with them.

In 2009 this caused the State Department to issue policy guidance, which in effect barred its 450 Education USA Advising Centres, who carry out a similar role as the British Council, from working with commercial recruitment agents. All the behaviours that they considered to be unethical are wholeheartedly embraced by UK universities. UK universities offer scholarship to specific agent's applicants, free travel for agents or influencers to visit the university, marketing stipends for the agents to use in-country and more. All this with the sole and stated aim to restrict the students' options to only their own university. But unlike in America, these are seen as legitimate tactics in the UK.

As well as the state frowning on the use of agents, the sector too had reservations. For many years the National Association of College Admission Counselling (NACAC), the most prominent association voice in admissions practices, banned the practice of using agents for international recruitment in its mandatory standards. Members who violated the standards were subject to exclusion from the association.

But in 2013, under pressure from universities, NACAC shifted their ban from mandatory to advisory. The floodgates were opened. In 'Using Agents to Recruit International Students: A Settled Issue?' Madeline Green says that 'in 2014 i-Graduate estimated that about a quarter of U.S. institutions were using agents; A year later, NACAC found that 37 percent of U.S. institutions were working with international student recruitment agencies, and an additional 20 percent were considering doing so' (Green 2017).

But it isn't all over.

As recently as 2017, the Middle States Commission on Higher Education proposed new language to its existing policy on recruitment that would prohibit Middle States-accredited institutions from using incentive-based compensation for recruiting international students.

UK UNIVERSITIES WORKING IN AMERICA

Due to the different drivers towards internationalisation, there are fundamental differences between international education administrators in UK universities and American ones. This can cause a clash of cultures that is the opposite of what one would expect. The brash salespeople of the UK international office are more akin to popular images of Americans than their more considered American counterparts.

American universities' international offices are more about assisting home students to study abroad and helping international students when they arrive on campus. In the majority of UK universities, UK international departments, are judged by commercial success, although there will be some element of outgoing study-abroad targets.

American universities prefer to have reciprocal agreements where they receive the same number of students as they send. There is no exchange of fees in this case and therefore no commercial drivers apart from trying not to lose the fees you already have.

However, this isn't what UK universities want, they do want places for their own students to study, and for some prestigious universities, this is the main driver, but for most post-1992 universities, this pales into insignificance against the need for fee income. Despite the US government's wishes, American universities see study abroad as a way of enabling their students to learn about other cultures and as a way to make their campuses more international rather than a matter of national security.

But actively recruiting UK universities see study abroad from America as a loss leader that can give access to fee-paying American students.

The success of this tactic is reflected in the fact that the UK is the number one study destination for American students but the 14th largest providers of incoming students. There are three times as many Americans that studied in the UK in 2016–17 than British that studied in America (IIE 2018).

NAFSA CONFERENCE

Since the days of Fred Flintstone, American business executives, salespeople and employees of large nationwide companies have held conventions. When the rest of the English-speaking world thought a convention meant a norm or rule and that to be unconventional was to be outside these rules, the Americans were developing a completely different meaning for the word. Masses of middle-aged, middle-class men would descend on holiday destinations for the annual convention. Drink would be had, bonding would occur, secretaries and PAs would be propositioned, romance may blossom, a few songs might be sung, happy salesmen would tap-dance on tables. Or at least that was how it was portrayed in numerous films. The rest of the world looked on slightly bemusedly.

Now conventions are the norm worldwide.

For UK universities that are keen to recruit American students, the convention to join is held by NAFSA each year. The NAFSA Conference brings the world's higher education industry together as no other. Each year has a theme, taken from some combination of the words global, internationalisation, leadership, partnership, new, studying and strategies.

There are over 10,000 professionals who attend from 350 countries. And to get noticed requires skill. Some do it by joining together to have a larger more obvious presence. Others host lavish parties – one of the best tickets in town is the Scottish universities' party which has been organised by a member of a Scottish new university for many years. There you may have the chance to chat with likeminded educators while you taste some whisky, then maybe an amuse bouche of haggis washed down with some whisky; as the night continues you could listen to some Scottish music while you taste some whisky, then as things warm up you may have a try at Scottish dancing while you try some whisky and then toast to the end of the night with some whisky. Of course, other alcoholic drinks are available.

One feels sorry for the Welsh universities that have a stand together. Their party – sorry reception – must be a dull affair; after all, Wales has no national drink, and their famous delicacies of leeks and boiled seaweed don't really travel well.

The point behind these affairs is to make connections while ensuring that you do not stray off the straight and narrow as determined by the ethical codes on study abroad. There can be no free trips to visit the UK offered unless there is some 'work' involved. Gifts should be tasteful but cheap. But it is all about connecting with the right people. NAFSA is different from a recruitment fair as you are there to influence the influencers as opposed to selling a programme to an individual. On top of that, as it is so large, it is a chance to meet up with partners from all over the world not just America. A better example of the connected international education world is harder to find.

GLASGOW CALEDONIAN UNIVERSITY (GCU), NEW YORK

One UK post-1992 university tried to be more direct and open its own campus. New York has 94 universities. Many are world class and many are not

(UNIPAGE 2019). In addition, it has numerous community colleges that also offer higher education programmes. In 2013 the management of Glasgow Caledonian University (GCU), a post-1992 university that consistently sits around 75th out of 130th in the UK rankings, felt that the city of New York was missing a university of their calibre.

So they decided to open a New York campus. The board of governors got out their traditional rubber stamp and approved the bold new move just as they had approved the campus in London. At least in New York, there was no chance that their operation would risk their highly trusted status in the same way that the London campuses could do as the students wouldn't be coming to Britain and wouldn't need visas.

The champagne was cracked open and the board looked forward to business class flights to New York on a regular basis. The only problem was no one had checked with the New York State Education Department what the regulations were for a foreign university to award degrees in the city. And actually, as no other foreign university had done so, the education department might not have been able to answer.

Press announcements followed, with a beaming principal announcing the first UK university to open a campus in New York. True to form, all hailed this as a triumph. Or those that did not, weren't given any airtime.

The senior staff and board of governors jetted off from 'the sick man of Europe' to the Big Apple.

There, the principal hosted an exclusive champagne reception for 250 guests in the Stephen Weiss Centre in the heart of the trendy Village.

It was all going so well, an expensive building in Manhattan was found and refitted at a cost of £2.5 million and a 15-year lease entered into.

A cross-party delegation of beaming Scottish politicians was invited to visit the new campus in early 2014, where the first minister at the time, Alex Salmond, gave the inaugural Caledonian Lecture. It fitted in with the Scottish government's drive to be seen on the world stage – as foreign policy was not a devolved issue. So they were fulsome in GCU's praise. No one in the delegation, or in the Scottish press, questioned whether this fitted in with the university's stated belief in the common good and of being a university that catered for local needs and prided itself in improving access for underprivileged students. But by 2016 even the Scottish press could ignore the fact that there had been an almighty and expensive cock-up. 'Glasgow Caledonian New York Campus in Turmoil Over US Based Objections', trumpeted the *Herald* as two New York universities formally objected to GCU being granted a licence (Hutcheson, 2016). 'New York Gets Tough Over Scottish University Invader' (Sanderson

2017), the *Times* picked up the story as it developed. Even the *Huffington Post* ran it: 'So Glasgow Caledonian University Has a Campus in New York. But There Are No Students' (Sherriff 2017).

By then it was clear that GCU had not understood the process they would have to go through to gain permission to award degrees as a private university. And there were mounting costs. There was the cost of the lease and refurbishment of a very expensive building in Manhattan. But in addition, the wages bill was eye-watering for a provincial university. Especially one which in 2011 had announced 95 redundancies in order to make 'essential' savings.

According to the *Herald* in 2018, 'Cara Smyth, who leads the team at GCU New York, is reported to be on a salary on £216,498, while Dean Bob Clougherty receives a salary topping £150,000' (Hutchinson 2016).

As the years dragged on and the costs continued without any income, the university doggedly stuck to its plan.

Eventually in 2017, after the university had spent £11.8 million, it was awarded provisional degree-awarding powers. This meant that for five years it cannot award degrees in its own name; instead successful students would be awarded degrees by the state authorities.

Even after the power to teach degrees was awarded, the campus failed to reach targets. In the first year it enrolled only 16 students. An article in the *Herald*, 'Glasgow Caledonian Income from Our New York Campus Is "Very Disappointing"', printed excerpts from the university's Finance and General Purposes Committee, which said, 'The Committee therefore had limited confidence in the 17/18 forecast budget previously provided for GCNYC or the likelihood that income streams would be realised. While the Committee noted that there might be reasons why income had not materialised, it could not accept continued and significant underachievement of budgeted income' (Hutchinson 2018).

However the university court approved a further £1.8 million to be made available to the campus, taking the total spend to £13.6 million. The argument for the low numbers in session 2017–18 was how late the license was awarded (June 2017). However in session 2018–19, the New York campus had only 58 students – considerably less than the projected numbers. In 2018, after poor recruitment, the court rubber-stamped another injection of cash and the principal 'noted' that the executive 'understood the concerns of Court members' (Hutchinson 2018). Hardly the words of someone having to strongly defend the loss of nearly £12 million.

The case of Glasgow Caledonian in New York shows all the themes that have run through this book. As described in the earlier chapters, the leaders of ex-polytechnics have a history of making strategic decisions as a reaction to competition with others in the sector. In a press report from GCU in 2012, where the decision to open a campus in New York was first announced, the principal pointed out that rival universities were dominating the TNE landscape in Scotland and ' if Glasgow Caledonian University is to progress positively in such a highly competitive environment, raising our international standing further is essential' (GCU 2012).

As shown earlier, the senior management in ex-polytechnics operate in an environment where the board of governors – in this case called the court is weak.

As with all post-1992 universities opening campuses overseas, the driver for opening a campus in New York was financial. No other argument would have sufficed for the court. In the same way as their campus in London, it was seen that attracting students to New York is an easier task than attracting them to Glasgow. In the first press report in 2012, it was mentioned that one of the aims was to attract students to the New York campus from Latin America (GCU 2012).

The American system is different, outwith for-profit providers, commercial drivers are not seen as paramount or even desirable. In GCU's submission to the New York State Education Department, the university tried to claim that it was driven by a 'defining social mission' which includes 'creating a better and fairer world' (Horne 2017). At the hearing, Joseph Muriana, vice president of Fordham University, the oldest Jesuit college in America ,'ridiculed the idea that Glasgow Caledonian was seeking to cater for poorer students, pointing to the $34,650 cost of their masters degrees' (Horne 2017).

As we have seen throughout this book, the British press do not hold the university sector to count. While they did highlight the financial costs and the mistakes made, at no time did they enter into a debate as to the morals and ethics of the venture as a whole. This was also the case with politicians.

It must be surprising to Americans because Glasgow Caledonian University, like the majority of universities in the UK, is a state university. In the year the campus was opened, over 80 per cent of the university's income came directly or indirectly from the government. There is no conceivable way in which a state university in America would contemplate opening a campus out of state to gain financial benefit. As Muriana pointed out in the hearing, 'An application from the University of Connecticut, or from Rutgers [in New Jersey] or UPenn [the University of Pennsylvania] to establish a campus in New York would be seen as absurd' (Horne 2017).

But the idea of education as an export is so deeply ingrained in the UK psyche that the press and politicians seldom, if ever, question whether universities funded through the public purse should have their strategic direction decided by the market.

In the UK, state-funded universities are applauded when they behave as private for-profit universities – especially if they do so overseas. It is only when this goes wrong as in the case of the London campuses and the GCU's New York campus that they are ever criticised.

In the American state university system, it is different. The state university system sees its role as providing an education for the inhabitants and industries of that state. Fees are less for students in state and more for out of state students. Campuses are deliberately spread throughout the state to ensure access to the system. Individual universities and colleges within the system are encouraged to attract outside funding, including from international students. But as we have seen, by limiting the use of agents and other legislation, they are discouraged from behaving like private for-profit organisations.

Thus, unlike London, New York and Washington are not awash with campuses from out-of-state universities whose role is to educate local students.

One may think that the New York campus saga was unique. However, there have been many other cases where UK universities have gone a long way down the route to opening campuses or entities overseas only to fall foul of national legislation.

CHAPTER 14

THE QUALITY ASSURANCE AGENCY
FOR HIGHER EDUCATION (QAA)

People outwith the higher education sector would be forgiven for thinking that the QAA's role is to regulate the sector and ensure standards. That, however, is not the case. The QAA is a system of self-regulation rather than an independent body. It is funded through subscriptions from higher education establishments and through contracts with major funding agencies. Most of the reviewers employed by the QAA to conduct reviews of universities are academics in other universities, which will themselves be reviewed.

When speaking to Innovation, Universities, Science and Skills Select Committee in 2009 (Students and Universities 2009), the QAA representative said,

> The primary responsibility for academic standards and quality rests with individual institutions. QAA reviews and reports on how well they meet those responsibilities, identifies good practice and makes recommendations for improvement. We visit institutions to conduct our audits, make judgements and publish reports, but we are not an inspectorate or a regulator and do not have statutory powers. We aim to ensure that institutions have effective processes in place to secure their academic standards, but we do not judge the standards themselves.

This concentration on processes rather than standards and quality has led to a scenario where as long as the processes are seen to be in place the boxes ticked, the QAA will give a good report. This was highlighted in a number of written responses to the committee (Students and Universities – Innovation, Universities, Science and Skills Committee Contents 2009).

Professor Geoffrey Alderman said, 'It is possible to come out of the QAA with a glowing report but in fact have poor standards'. Others noted that 'each department or faculty assesses the "quality" of its own course, but this assessment is usually merely an examination of the course documentation'. Dr Fenton, an academic, went a step further by saying that the QAA was 'another bureaucratic, administrative burden that you learn to play the game of' (Students and Universities 2009).

The committee was not impressed with the QAA in terms of how it worked and its lack of autonomy. It stated, 'We do not accept that sound processes necessarily denote high quality. That is the trap that many bureaucracies and those that run them fall into.' They felt that the QAA leaving universities to decide on standards meant that it was toothless and that things were so bad that there was 'a justifiable case for recommending the abolition of the QAA and starting afresh with a new body'. However, they were worried about the disruption that would cause and so recommended instead that the QAA should be reformed and re-established as a quality and standards agency. It would be formed by a royal charter and be responsible by statute for standards of university education and would monitor and report on standards to the Parliament. It would be funded through HEFCE to maintain independence. The committee finished by saying:

> In making these recommendations we are looking to see a fundamental change in the operation of the QAA and that, if this cannot be achieved within two years, the QAA/Quality and Standards Agency should be abolished and an entirely new organisation be established in its place. (Students and Universities 2009)

The higher education sector ignored the committee's recommendation at the time and it has not been enacted since. In fact, the new Office for Students has outsourced its quality function to the QAA.

But all the criticisms by the committee can be seen in the way the QAA has managed the development of TNE worldwide. The speed with which TNE activities developed and changed to fit in with the changes in the host country caused the QAA problems. As universities became more entrepreneurial, the QAA was always behind the curve.

In 1999 they published a section (Section 2) of their Code of Practice on Collaborative Arrangements. The code consisted of a list of guiding principles named 'precepts' relating to maintenance of academic quality in collaborative relationships. It was up to individual universities to set up their own systems to ensure they were following these precepts and the QAA published guidelines to help them do so.

Post-1992 universities, like their pre-1992 peers, had a mixed reaction to the risks involved in collaboration. But as ex-polytechnics, they had memories of the more heavy-handed regime of the CNAA, which had validated their degrees before they gained degree-awarding powers themselves. Some still felt the shadows of a system which at the start had been unashamedly 'quality control'. Thus it was more likely that the quality function in post-1992 universities was more powerful and restrictive than its pre-1992 counterparts who had never had an external quality body overseeing them. Internal battles between a small group of usually fairly junior quality staff and senior staff who had their sights on world domination raged throughout the sector. Discussions, debates and arguments raged over the adverbs that the QAA used in its reports. It didn't help that the QAA as a system of self-regulation attempted to keep any criticism as minimal as possible. It always started with examples of good practices and hid criticism with mealy words, the most damning was when they 'strongly recommended' something.

In 2004 the collaborative section was updated to replace the precepts and guidance on how to maintain the precepts by precepts and explanation. One can only imagine the torturous debates that must have gone on before this momentous change came about.

At that time the majority of collaborative work that was being carried out was by universities teaching their programmes overseas, often with private colleges, and the precepts were based around these models.

Words of wisdom such as 'There should be a written and legally binding agreement or contract setting out the rights and obligations of the parties and signed by the authorised representatives of the awarding institution and the partner organisation or agent', were followed by a list of sections that should be in the contract and duly copied by legal departments throughout the land. Lists of questions that should be answered in a due diligence check were given, causing boxes to be ticked all over the world. Being British, these were designed with a view to working with a more junior foreign partner and caused some dismay when one worked with a high-ranking overseas partner who had to prove that they were solvent, wouldn't engage in corruption and had proper Western educational values. It also caused problems when working in less developed countries, where one had to determine that the laboratories would be safe for students and staff and that the partner had correct HR processes in place. But there were always ways to get round these things as long as the senior staff in the university wanted to have their own graduation ceremonies in exotic locations. And, of course, the QAA only wanted to ensure that you had systems in place and that you understood the system. So as long as you asked if there was a health and safety policy, it didn't matter if you were told no and then still went ahead – you had followed the system the question asked and the box was ticked.

There was only one precept that dealt with joint awards in 1999, and in the revised version of 2004 in the explanation section, the code stated, 'Despite the collaborative nature of the study, responsibility for each award, and its academic standard, remains with the body awarding it and cannot be shared between the partners' (Quality Assurance Agency for Higher Education 2004). It was made plain to quality officers throughout the land that the QAA frowned on joint awards and would rather that UK universities steered clear of them certainly outwith Europe.

But with the explosion of joint awards in China and Malaysia, the QAA could not keep up with reality.

In 2010 they brought out another version of the code for collaborative, which was called 'an amplification'. This was an admission that UK universities had already developed processes that were widely different from those that the QAA had envisaged. In the 'amplification', the QAA admitted that a 'one size fits all' approach could no longer be used and that many collaborations were now leading to dual of joint awards (Quality Assurance Agency for Higher Education 2010). It tried to find a way of acknowledging that it had not had enough guidance for dual and joint awards while realising that most UK universities had gone ahead and created them anyway. When they visited China to carry out reviews, they specifically missed out reviewing articulations. This was because they knew that the vast majority of MOE approved joint degrees and were being called articulations at home and they didn't want to open that can of worms. When they did review the few programmes where the UK award was given in China as part of a joint award, they merely noted the different ways that these operated.

By 2015 they came out with a document, 'Characteristic Statement: Qualifications Involving More Than One Degree Awarding Body', which acknowledged that they were far behind the curve. It stated: 'The purpose of this document is to provide information about the types and characteristics of qualifications involving more than one degree-awarding body. It aims to help build a common understanding of these arrangements and highlight typical approaches to quality assurance, which enable academic standards to be set and maintained where degree awarding powers are pooled' (Quality Assurance Agency for Higher Education 2015). In this document, they admitted that even though they only were set up to look at the processes that universities went through to develop and run collaborations and not standards, they had failed to do even that.

CHAPTER 15

THE AUGAR REVIEW

Only when the idea of a free market opened up domestically did the government begin to question whether universities could be trusted to operate ethically and in the national interest in a free market, despite the fact that they had been operating in a free market internationally for decades. The Augar Review of higher education returned its recommendations in 2019 (Augar 2019). Seen as an attempt by the May government to offset the statements from Labour that they would abolish fees, it was published just as May announced her resignation.

In part, the review is an acknowledgement that leaving universities to operate in a free market has not worked. And so the review recommended that the government should return to some form of fiscal control over the sector. As the report says, 'competition has an important role to play in creating student choice, but, with no steer from government, the social, economic and cultural outcomes are likely to be suboptimal'. The review states that 'undirected funding has led to an over-supply of some courses at great cost to the taxpayer and a corresponding undersupply of graduates in strategically important sectors. We believe government should have greater control over taxpayer support to higher education.'

The Augar Review condemns many of the aggressive tactics that UK universities have used in the domestic market. A look at the perpetrators of these tactics shows that post-1992 universities are at the forefront. This should not be a surprise as they are the ones that struggle most to attract students. But of course this does not mean that some pre-1992 universities don't behave as badly.

Since the introduction of fees in England, post-1992 universities used some of the same aggressive methods that they had pioneered overseas. This resulted in grade inflation, lower entry requirements and unconditional offers which the review interpreted as 'consequences of market competition'.

It is interesting to contrast how UK universities have behaved when they started charging fees with American universities who have always charged fees. American domestic fees are the most important element of universities' funding, particularly for smaller and less well-known colleges. But there has been no need for an American version of the Augar Report.

American universities have always been in competition for fee income. But their regulatory bodies and attitude to the morals of how to compete were developed within the domestic market, unlike the UK where competition overseas developed before it was translated to the domestic market. Thus, there is a healthy debate in the higher education sector in America around the ethics of using commercial tactics to recruit students. For instance, it is only recently that the use of agents has become widespread and there is new legislation against third party providers.

GRADE INFLATION

In the UK in the five years since the introduction of fees from 2012/13 to 2016/17, the number of students who gained a first class degree increased from 18 per cent to 26 per cent. Of the ten worst offenders, those who had the largest increase in firsts over the period, five were post-1992 and the other five were plate glass universities (Richmond 2018). According to a report by the think tank Reform, this was a deliberate effort on behalf of UK universities to attract fees (Richmond 2018). It says,

In a 2015 paper on grade inflation in UK universities, Ray Bachan from the University of Brighton pointed out that ' "there may be a conscious effort by UK universities to lower the "hedonistic" price by lowering standards to attract fee paying students'. Professor Geoffrey Alderman observed back in 2010 that there were already 'intolerable pressures on academic staff to pass students who should rightfully fail and to award higher classes of degrees to the undeserving'. A survey of over 2,000 academics in 2015 found that almost half of them had recently experienced pressure to bump up student grades or stop students failing […] the evidence above lends further weight to the notion that universities are not as willing as one might hope to protect quality and standards, particularly when league tables and tuition fees are so high on their agenda. (Richmond 2018)

And as mentioned in an earlier chapter, the QAA does not see its role as deciding on standards of university degrees.

There is little evidence to show whether grade inflation happened with international students – although this is because there has been little research into the phenomenon.

However, in the case of international students, the pressures to award degrees are not just institutional but personal. When students fail to attain enough credits to be awarded a degree, there are often serious personal implications.

For international students, this is not just a case of 'come back next year and do a resit'. Visa issues do not allow part-time attendance and so at the very least a full year would have to be re-sat. But for most international students in UK universities, failing is extremely serious and they are desperate not to have to return home having failed.

If they fail, Chinese students, often the only child in their family would lose face. Nigerian, Indian or Pakistani students often have used up their family's life savings for the opportunity of a Western education.

So all beat a path to module leaders, programme leaders, heads of Department, deans of international, even eventually the principal, until they are offered a solution.

ENTRY STANDARDS

The Augar Review showed that there had been an increase in students with lower prior qualifications entering universities and felt that this was due to market forces. While it welcomed the opportunities this afforded students, it worried that the progression rate was poor. 'At fourteen UK universities, projections of the number of students likely to obtain a degree is below 70 per cent; the lowest has a degree projection rate of 51.7 per cent.'

The notion that universities would take students into qualifications that they had a high possibility to fail purely for funding was implied.

Whether this is the case or not, it is a fact that once number controls were lifted, prestigious universities lowered their entry requirements to take more students at the expense of less prestigious ones. The UCAS end-of-cycle report for 2015 found that in the 2015 intake, Russell Group and other selective universities increased their intakes by 7 per cent. The report revealed that to do this they lowered their entry requirements. Lower tariff universities only managed a 0.7 per cent increase in numbers (UCAS 2015).

This is a pattern that has been seen with the UK. As markets mature and pre-1992 universities expand into them, competition develops where even prestigious universities lower their entry requirements. In most markets, league tables are believed to be a true reflection of the quality of a university. In all UK league tables, post-1992 universities hold the bottom places. In the *Complete University Guide*, the lowest 60 are all post-1992; in the *Guardian* the bottom 50. This means that they find it difficult to compete with universities significantly higher up the tables and as these universities lower their entry requirements, post-1992 universities have had to follow suit. However, there is only so far that they can go, so as markets mature, post-1992 universities are pushed out of them.

UNCONDITIONAL OFFERS

The rise in unconditional offers to students who have not actually sat their A levels is a broader indication of how UK universities react to competition. From less than 3,000 offers made in 2013, this has risen to nearly 70,000 in 2018. Which means that nearly 23 per cent of all applicants are receiving unconditional offers. The Universities Minister Sam Gyimah called it irresponsible and that universities that were offering these unconditional offers to 18-year olds had a 'bums on seat' mentality (Busby 2018). Education Minister Damian Hinds said that it was 'unacceptable for universities to adopt pressure selling tactics' (Busby 2019). He labelled the use of unconditional closed offers – those where the student is given an unconditional offer only if they accept the place as their first choice as 'unethical'. Of course, it is those universities that are most desperate for bums on seats that were the worst offenders with 20 universities making up 70 per cent of all unconditional offers made. Of these, one, Nottingham University said it would stop the practice immediately. Of the remaining 22, 18 are post-1992 universities, with the others, including a Russell Group University, claiming to make the offers only to 'high achievers'. Even Universities UK found it hard to give a robust defence of the practice, merely stating that if used wisely, they are a valuable admissions tool.

The Augar Review documents a catalogue of dubious practices that UK universities and in particular post-1992 universities have been engaged in since fees were set at £9,000 in 2012. But, in fact, they had been working in a market-led environment overseas for decades, with little or no regulation, examination or direction. Successful UK government international strategies have set targets for numbers of full fee-paying students and more recently TNE students. This has always been couched in commercial terms. UK universities' experience of chasing full-fee students overseas created organisations that developed innovative and flexible ways to attract students. Agents were paid large incentive bonuses, given trips abroad and wooed to ensure that they sold one university over another – some were even allowed to make admission decisions. Fees were discounted heavily under the pretence that the student had gained a scholarship. Large-scale marketing campaigns were paid for. Entry requirements including English language were 'flexible'.

This was translated rapidly into how they chased domestic fees. However, at home the commercial behaviour of universities is under more scrutiny. Fundamentally this has led to an increasing distrust of universities and questions as to whether they are working in the national interest.

While much has been made of this in the press and the Augar Report, no one has looked into how the same universities have been operating the commercial environment overseas, let alone question if the quality of full-fee-paying students they allow into the country has had an effect, either good or bad, on academic standards and output for home students.

CHAPTER 16

FINAL

THE MYTH THAT UNIVERSITIES ARE ALL EQUAL

The prevailing argument given by media, politicians and the higher education sector is that we have a world-class higher education system and that includes all universities.

The depth of the belief of a single higher education sector is surprising, given that in reality we all have a notion of which universities are best and this is reinforced by league tables and other metrics. PMI did much to advance the view of a single sector by lumping all UK universities under a single brand, Education@UK.

But there was already a wish for it to be a fact. When post-1992 universities were given their charters, all political parties saw the binary divide as being a form of discrimination. This was as a direct result of the funding difference between both sides of the divide. The polytechnic side of the divide, with poorer funding, was more working class compared to the universities' populations.

So now, any attempt to discuss post-1992 universities as a separate entity are seen as subversive and backwards. If one expresses the belief that post-1992 universities should be treated as different, it is seen as a wish to return to a system where there were two classes of universities.

Debate is suppressed by making it different to make comparisons. For instance, the British Council's interactive student data mining tool has grouped together Russell Group Universities, the Million Plus Group, the 1994 Group and Alliance HE, which allows for comparisons between the groups to be made. But there is no grouping for post-1992 universities. Likewise, in a report on the value of TNE to the UK, the same groupings were used, despite the fact that some of the largest providers of TNE are in none of the groupings (Department BIS, 2017).

The lack of debate stems from the belief that the binary divide was designed to deliberately create two classes of universities, which was a barrier to meritocracy. However, that was not the purpose of the binary divide. It was

149

actually the opposite; the binary divide was intended to emulate the European system where vocational higher education was seen on par with academic higher education. Thus the development of polytechnics arose from a need for the UK to develop a vocational sector with equal esteem as academic. This never came about. Polytechnics were underfunded compared to universities. And as Augar points out, the further-education sector was treated even worse.

Some 1992 universities developed programmes that could be considered to be vocational, and employability of graduates is now a factor which is measured. But that does not mean that vocational education even in pre-1992 universities has parity of esteem. A quick look through the senior civil service shows that the most senior civil servant in the Scottish office studied music, the most senior in Wales studied French literature and Northern Ireland history, an economist is in charge of railways, the head of intelligence studied English literature and so on. In most cases it is hard to find where the heads of civil service departments actually had skills in the area that they were head of. And, of course, that counts even more for ministers. Since the polytechnics started, we have had 10 prime ministers out of which seven studied at Oxford, one at Edinburgh and only two did not have any university education. There may no longer be a distinct binary divide but that does not mean that all universities are equal. For most onlookers, there seems to be a more layered system, with Oxbridge and some ancient universities at the top and ex-polytechnics at the bottom.

The desire to have parity between vocational and academic streams has been a mantra of politicians of all hues over the decades, from Wilson in the 1960sto May in 2019. Prime ministers, mainly graduates of Oxbridge, have stood in front of the cameras, and with serious faces said that they will no longer tolerate the notion that a vocational education is inferior to an academic one. They have then turned to their Oxbridge educated parliamentary private secretaries and asked them to sort something out that doesn't cost any money. Not surprisingly, none has developed or funded a proper strategy, and parity of esteem has not followed.

That being said, despite underfunding and top-heavy boards of governance, polytechnics were different than universities and fulfilled a different mission.

They maintained the part-time route in higher education, were remarkably successful in expanding sandwich course provision and also expanded in business and social sciences. They achieved a major shift towards degree courses and a substantial expansion at postgraduate level, though at the cost of stagnation of sub-degree work. Polytechnics expanded access to new kinds of students. They were particularly successful in increasing number of women, students from ethnic minorities and mature students. They maintained greater access to students from working-class backgrounds, though less than might have been hoped for. More than half of degree entrants had non-traditional qualifications.

A higher proportion of their graduates than those from universities entered employment, particularly in engineering and manufacturing (Pratt 1997).

Directors of polytechnics had assured government that when they gained university status, they would keep the polytechnics' distinct mission.

But when they joined the ranks of universities, they felt that they would get a 'fair share' of the funding. However, it became apparent that this would not be the case. Many ex-polytechnics reckoned that in order to get access to research funds and more non-exchequer income, they would have to be seen as the same as those research-intensive universities they were competing with. But almost none have been successful, and they are still being funded less and seen as a second choice by students after pre-1992 universities. The average entry requirements for programmes in pre-1992 universities is higher than post-1992 ones for almost all programmes (Institute for Employment Research 2012). The bottom rungs of all UK university rankings are taken up by post-1992 universities, and worldwide it is understood that they are second choice. Where we can find information, it is clear that post-1992 universities have lower entry requirements and less benefits from their qualifications. The Augar Review found that most institutions which have graduates with a negative graduate premium, that is, the increase in salary they command as graduates is not enough to offset the fees they pay, are in the post-1992 sector.

With the change to university status, most of what made polytechnics different was lost. But it wasn't replaced with anything that made them unique and, some may say, relevant. Post-1992 universities attempt to define themselves individually. They are Ambitious at Heart, Life Changing, they Stand Ready and are for the Common Weal – whatever that is. They are places where you can Realise Your Ambitions, or Go Your Own Way. You could be invited to Join Our Tribe! University Begins With You. But the fact cannot be hidden that they have drifted into becoming poorer versions of their pre-1992 counterparts.

The polytechnic experiment was doomed by underfunding and over-management with unwieldy boards of governance and the desire of their senior management to become part of the existing university sector.

But the real nail in the coffin was the lack of a farsighted strategy to make a fundamental change to the education system. The polytechnic sector was set up in industrial cities in a post-industrial Britain. It continued to have a traditional view of vocational qualifications as people who worked for industry – although it added some new vocations such as business studies and computing. What it failed to do was to redefine vocational studies. There are no qualifications more vocational than doctors, lawyers, dentists, vets, religious ministers and others who work out with manufacturing industry. If the funding and staff to train these vocations had been transferred into the polytechnic sector, it would have changed the status of vocational qualifications – and still could. One heartening recent development is the creation of five new medical schools in England, all of which are either located in post-1992 universities or in partnership with post-1992 universities.

SENIOR MANAGEMENT

The story, post-polytechnic was one of an increase in power of senior staff who ensured that they had toothless boards of governors. The nature of the relationship among ex-polytechnics was developed as a competitive one rather than a collaborative one. Size was the measure of success. The rise of the principal or vice chancellor as a CEO created a group of universities where the senior staff act as if the university belongs to them. Management structures oscillate around centralised control, decentralised control, matrix management, bad management and so on as each new VC feels the need to put their stamp on 'their' university. The post-1992 sector seldom has a collegiate feel and many pre-1992 universities have followed this model to some extent. The rise of the principal as CEO has allowed some post-1992 universities to make financial decisions that are not scrutinised well enough. It is no surprise that two of the UK universities that lost their visa sponsorship status had significant financial problems which could be attributed to a mixture of aggressive commercial behaviour by their principals and weak governance.

Universities UK is accepted by the press and media as the voice of the sector, but is in fact the voice of the principals and vice chancellors of universities in the same way as the committee of directors of polytechnics (CDP) was the voice of the leaders of polytechnics. As mentioned earlier, CDP lobbied to deliberately create a sector which had toothless boards of governors and their members had high salaries and total control. Universities UK has a similar role. That is why the 'voice of UK universities' routinely defends VC salaries, and the fact that many VCs are on their own remuneration committees and come out with statements such as universities 'recommend that the cap in fees be abolished' and claim that that is view of the whole university. These opinions are presented as the view of the university community as a whole rather than a small section of senior staff.

Perhaps this is because unions are no longer representative of the majority of staff and there is no credible alternative voice.

For there to be a real debate within the sector, there needs to be another voice that canvasses the views of all stakeholders. A voice that is heard by the mainstream press. The governance structure of post-1992 universities is protected by Universities UK even though it is not the norm throughout the world. This is no surprise because it gives a great deal of power to the university principals who make up the membership of Universities UK. In many countries and indeed in some UK universities, senior staff are voted in for a fixed period of time. In others the staff of the university have control of the board of governors. One only has to look at the cooperative university in Mondragon in Spain to see a successful university which is run as a cooperative for the benefit of the staff, students and community. Some may mention that it is not high in world league tables but that should not be the ambition of every university.

POST-1992 UNIVERSITIES WORKING INTERNATIONALLY

UK universities, including post-1992 universities, work all over the world in areas where they make a real difference. Teaching teachers in Palestine, working with micro-banks in India, educating nurses and health care workers worldwide, teams of academics and administrators have gained funding from governments and NGOs to use their skills to help others.

However, these are a small part of most UK universities' international activities. Their main effort has been in commercially exploiting international students.

Polytechnics and then post-1992 universities did the heavy lifting in the massification of UK higher education. They took more students and taught them for less money than their pre-1992 counterparts. But eventually efficiency gains were not enough to ensure that the system was adequately funded. So the government encouraged UK universities to look for funding outwith government sources. With PMI, all were encouraged to look at the recruitment of international students as a commercial venture. The reduction of international students to targets endorsed by the UK governments has meant that they are treated as a commodity and not as young people making the most important decision of their life as many are. Rather than counselling and guiding them to the educational experience that is best suited to their abilities, they are harassed and cajoled by agents and recruitment teams into any universities desperate to meet targets – all watched by admiring media and government agencies who laud the fact that education is now one of the largest exports in the UK.

The use of agents is not questioned and is even condoned by the British Council. If private companies started up in the UK with the sole aim to persuade a British youngster to spend huge amounts of money on a programme of study with no compulsion to give all the possible options available to that young person, surely someone would object. Especially if those companies were being given extensive incentives to persuade youngsters to choose a particular university or even programme over others that may be more suitable. And as for the situation where many of these agents were authorised to make offers, where was Universities UK? – In all consultations they have made it plain that it should be universities that are the sole arbiters of admission to university.

There seems to be a view that these behaviours are allowable with foreign students.

At home, there was no coherent government-led strategy for the internationalisation of higher education. There was no plan to ensure that this influx of international students and increasing international experience of academics was to be used for the national good – to give home students an international education. While other countries, China, Malaysia, Sweden, Denmark, Poland and others, developed strategies that would ensure that their universities developed home students who had an international education, the UK did not. And UK Universities have helped these other countries develop higher education systems that internationalise their own students without any educational benefits to UK students.

For post-1992 universities, by far the largest source of non-exchequer funding was from international students but they had the hardest sell and sold the hardest, taking more risks. It is no surprise that only post-1992 universities have had problems with their visa sponsorship status.

As they had done in the massification of UK higher education post-1992 universities took to the notion of competition with a vengeance, undercutting each other in terms of entry requirements, fees and payments to third parties. In the UK, post-1992 universities pride themselves in accepting students with lower and different academic qualifications and have developed systems to help these students study at degree level. This experience was transferred overseas. Many used the post-study work visa, which allowed students to work in the UK as a way of attracting students who could not afford the fees to come to the UK and work to pay back loans that they had taken.

The pool of students they attracted was thus poorer academically and poorer financially than those attracted by the majority of pre-1992 universities.

This has resulted in them being hit harder when there are economic problems in country or tightening of visa controls in the UK.

Within days of Boris Johnston becoming prime minister, he reintroduced post-study work visa and increased targets for international students. Despite the fact that almost all non-Scottish universities charge £9,000 fees for home students and most would be considered well-funded in world terms, they are still likely to use this new visa system to trawl the world for students who cannot afford the fees, encouraging them to take out loans to pay for their education and promising them that they will be able to earn enough in unskilled jobs to pay them back.

MEDIA SCRUTINY

Since the formation of post-1992 universities, the media look on at the whole 170 universities in the UK benevolently and seldom look underneath the veneer of middle-class politeness and superiority that the universities arm themselves with. They do a good job of highlighting specific problems with particular universities or senior staff. But on the whole they do not question the behaviour of the university sector in general. Despite Augar, no one seriously questions whether it is the place of UK universities, mainly funded by the state, to teach programmes overseas, which have little positive academic effect on home students. Or if the amount of money spent by international students, often from very poor families, is warranted or justified by the results and education they receive.

Almost any behaviour carried out overseas is heralded as good news rather than scrutinised. When GCU opened its campus in New York, it was lauded. The operation of London campuses, purely to attract income from international students, was only questioned when there were significant problems identified. And even then, the damning report from the QAA on the operation of London campuses was largely ignored. Universities opening campuses overseas is only ever considered a good thing, as is UK universities' TNE, no matter if they are in Dubai, where British academics have been imprisoned, or in China in the same cities as so-called re-education centres or Myanmar while it carries out ethnic cleansing.

A MULTILAYERED UNIVERSITY SECTOR

Apart from there being little oversight from boards of governors in post-1992 universities, there has been a lessening of control from the state.

Before caps were abolished, there were attempts, by using funding for quotas, to ensure that the sector prioritised subjects deemed to be in the nation's interests. However, by introducing international students, UK universities could ignore national interests. In subjects where there were quotas, if you wished to increase numbers you would be given less government funding per student. But universities could still expand without lessening their unit of funding by recruiting international students. For post-1992 universities, in particular, this meant that business schools became larger and larger.

In subjects, such as STEM subjects, where universities found it difficult to fill quotas with UK students, they actively recruited in Europe to fill their quotas, as

EU students were treated as home students. This meant they were filling places that were considered to be in subjects the country needed to train more people in, with European students rather than UK ones. It is little wonder that we need to turn to Europe to find qualified staff in many areas such as the National Health Service (NHS).

By these measures, the quota system was undermined and universities developed a shape and size unrelated to national interests and which was dictated by international competition and market forces. To an enquiry by the All Party Parliamentary Group for International Students, Universities UK made a virtue of this stating that, 'Many universities supplied us with lists of courses which would be unviable without international students. These ranged from four at one locally focused institution, to 67 at another specialist London-based institution, and nearly a third of courses at an institution with one of the highest levels of international students.'

The internationalisation of post-1992 universities has made a fundamental change to them. Home students have an opportunity to meet other young people from around the world. Academics and administrators have learnt much about working on an international scale. Local communities have had overseas money spent on them. And crucially, universities have been able to spend the money received on better facilities and resources. But are these benefits enough to continue to encourage all universities to operate unquestioned in the international market?

League tables prove that parts of the UK higher education sector are some of the best in the world. But those league tables are based on academic outputs not for outputs that meet national needs. In 2019 Germany and France did not have a single university in the top 40 of the THES World Rankings. Can we really say that the UK higher education system is creating better engineers and technocrats than their systems?

With Brexit looming large, whatever it looks like, the UK is going to have a new position in the world. It will need more internationally competent graduates and it will need to be able to produce graduates that meet local needs.

The narrative that higher education in the UK is a single sector is a barrier to a proper review of how we can develop a university sector that is best for individuals and the country as a whole. This must look at governance, funding and find new ways in which vocational education is considered equal in worth to non-vocational. It has long been argued by universities that they must have total freedom. This need for freedom from government interference may be true of some universities and allow them to carry out research that may have uncomfortable results for those in power. But it does not have to be true for all universities. Developing a tiered sector of higher education with each tier having different goals and priorities should not be allowed to be dismissed by a small group consisting of VCs and principals who would see it as a loss of status.

The Augar Review shows that the free market is no way to allow the university sector to operate. It has failed to (1) improve access for disadvantaged groups (2) attain parity for vocational higher education and (3) develop a lower technician-level education that is on par with our European neighbours. To do so requires a rethinking of the notion that higher education is a single 'world-class' sector. And indeed, we should disabuse ourselves of the belief that league tables are the method by which we decide the quality of our higher education sector.

We must open the debate and not shy away from a realistic appraisal of our higher education system, which acknowledges its weaknesses along with its strengths.

BIBLIOGRAPHY

Sixth Malaysia Plan. 1991. 'The Sixth Malaysian Plan'. https://policy.asiapacificenergy. org/node/1277 (accessed 2 December 2019).

Abraham Lincoln Commission on Study Abroad. 2005. 'Global Competencies and National Needs'. https://www.nafsa.org/policy-and-advocacy/policy-resources/ report-commission-abraham-lincoln-study-abroad-fellowship-program (accessed 2 December 2019).

Age of the Sage. n.d. https://www.age-of-the-sage.org/scientist/snow_two_cultures. html (accessed 21 November 2018).

Alexander, Bryan. 2019. 'College Closures Casulties of the Future and Queen Sacrifices'. 26 February. https://bryanalexander.org/horizon-scanning/casualties-of-the-future-college-closures-and-queen-sacrifices/ (accessed 26 May 2019).

Altbach, Philip. 2011. 'Abolish Agents and Third Party Recruiters'.University World News, 16 January.

Augar, Philip. 2019. *Review of Post 18 Educationn and Funding*.Review, Department of Education, 30 May. London: UK Government.

Aziz, Fazleena. 2016. 'International Student Enrolment up by 12 Percent Last Year: Higher Education Ministry'.*New Straits Times*, 30 March. https://www.nst. com.my/news/2016/03/136247/international-student-enrolment-12-percent-last-year-higher-education-ministry (accessed 21 February 2019).

BBC. 2012. 'Damian Green on London Metroplolitan Student Visas'. *BBC Today.* London, 30 August.

———. 2014a. 'Glyndwr University's Foreign Student Recruitment Freeze'. *BBC News.* 24 June.

———. 2014b. 'Student Visa System Fraud Exposed in BBC Investigation'. *BBC Panorama.* London, 10 February.

BBC News. 2004. 'Visa Move to Beat Population Drop'. London: BBC. 25 February.

BBC on This Day. 1967. 'De Gaulle Says 'non' to Britain – Again'. http://news.bbc. co.uk/onthisday/hi/dates/stories/november/27/newsid_4187000/4187714.stm (accessed 13 January 2020).

Bennett, Brian. 2002. 'The New Style of Board of Governonrs – Are They Working?' *Higher Education Quarterly*, 56, no. 3: 287–302.

Bingchen, Yao. 2015. Speech at the Sino Australia Forum on Transnational Education. 27 March, Beijing. https://internationaleducation.gov.au/International-network/china/PolicyUpdates-China/Documents/English%20translation%20of%20MOE%20DG%20Cen%20Jianjun%20opening%20address%20on%20TNE%20Forum.pdf (accessed 14 January 2020).

Black, K. 2004. 'A Review of Factors which Contribute to the Intetnationalisation of a Programme of Study'.*Journal of Hospitality, Leisure,Sport and Tourism Education*, vol. 3, no 1.

Bohm, Anthony, M. Follari, A. Hewett, S. Jones, N. Kemp, D. Meares, D. Pearce and K. Van Cauter. 2004. 'Vision 2020: Forecasting International Student Mobility: A UK Perspective'. British Council, Universities UK, IDP Education Australia and Education UK. https://www.britishcouncil.org/sites/default/files/vision-2020.pdf (accessed 2 December 2019).

Borden, David. 1991. 'National Security Education Act'. *Select Committee on Intellegence.* 4 December. https://www.intelligence.senate.gov/laws/david-l-boren-national-security-education-act-1991 (accessed 15 May 2019).

Bothwell, Ellie. 2015. 'Post-Study Work Options Main Reason for International Students Rejecting UK'. THES, 15 September.

Brady, Peter. 2006. 'Are We Training Others to Take Our Jobs'. March

———. 2013. 'Cameron Pits a Dynamic Education System against Ivory Tower Elitism'. *The Herald*, 12 March. http://www.heraldscotland.com/comment/columnists/cameron-pits-a-dynamic-education-system-against-ivory-tower-elitism.20658689 (accessed 2 December 2019).

———. 2016. 'World Of Opportunity'. *Professional Engineer* March.

British Council. 1999. 'Building a World Class Brand for British Education: The Brand Report'. London: British Council.

———. 2016. 'Malaysia Country Brief'. London: British Council.

———. 2016. The Scale and Scope of UK Higher Education, Trans National Education. June. https://www.britishcouncil.org/sites/default/files/scale-and-scope-of-uk-he-tne-report.pdf (accessed 29 November 2019).

Busby, Eleanor. 2018.'Universities Standards Under Question as Quarter of Teenagers Given Unconditional Offers'. *The Independant*, 26 July.

———. 2019. 'Universities Urged to Stop Using "Unethical"Tactics to Pressure Students into Accepting Offers'. *The Independant*, 5 April.

Cameroon, David. 2010. Prime Minister's Speech on Immigration on 10 October. https://www.gov.uk/government/speeches/prime-ministers-speech-on-immigration (accessed 30 November 2019).

Chai, Ho Chan. 2007. 'The Business of Higher Education'.*Comonwealth Educational Partnerships*: 114–18.

Chapman, James. 2010. 'Labour's Betrayal of British Workers: Nearly Every One of 1.67m Jobs Created since 1997 Has Gone to a Foreigner'. *Daily Mail*, 8 April.

Chiba, Keiko. 2010. 'A Future on Track'. *Financial Times*, 23 September.

Clarke, Charles. 2014. 'Register of Learning Providers'. *HC Deb 18 June 2004 vol 422 cc61-2WS*. London: Hansard 18 June 2004.

Cameron, David. 2010. 'A Contract between the Conservative Party and You'. Speech in April. http://www.fmotl.com/concon/Contract.htm (accessed 29 November 2019).

Congress. 2003. 'National Security Education Programme Report to United States Congress'. Report to Congress. http://congressionalresearch.com/RL31643/document.php (accessed 2 December 2019).

CPC Central Committee. 1995. '9th Five Year Plan'.*National Economy and Social Development and Long-Range Objectives to the Year 2010*. Beijing, 28 September.

Crosland, Tony. 1965. 'Text of Tony Croslands Woolwich Speech'.HEPI Higher Education Policy Institute. https://www.hepi.ac.uk/wp-content/uploads/2016/08/Scan-158.pdf (accessed 10 November 2018).

Crosland, Susan. 1982. *Tony Crosland*. London: Jonathon Cope.

Dearing, Ronald. 1997. 'Higher Education in the Learning Society'. Her Majesty's Stationery Office. http://www.educationengland.org.uk/documents/dearing1997/dearing1997.html (accessed 2 December 2019).

Dept. of Education, Dept. of International Trade. 2019. 'International Education Strategy: Global Potential, Global Growth'. March. https://www.gov.uk/government/publications/international-education-strategy-global-potential-global-growth (accessed 2 December 2019) and https://www.gov.uk/government/publications/international-education-strategy-global-potential-global-growth/international-education-strategy-global-potential-global-growth (accessed 10 April 2019).

Department BIS. 2017. The Wider Benefits of Transnational Education to the UK'. Research report July 2017. https://assets.publishing.service.gov.uk/government/uploads/system/uploads/attachment_data/file/624364/CRAC_TNE_report_final.pdf (accessed 14 January 2020).

Salehi-Sangari, E., and T. Foster. 1999. 'Curriculum Internationalisation, A Comparative Study in Iran and Sweden'. *European Journal of Marketing*, vol 33: 128.

Erasmus. 2017. *Erasmus Plus*. 17 June. https://www.erasmusplus.org.uk/statistics (accessed 20 June 2019).

Farnham, D., and S. Horton.1992. 'Human Resource Management in the Public Sector Leading or Following the Private Sector'. 22nd Annual Conference Public Administration Committee. New York: University of York.

Fisher, Karen. 2008. 'Code of Ethics for Study Abroad Is Offered to Colleges and Providers'. *Chronicle of Higher Education*. 3 March.

Ford, Richard. 2004. 'Bogus Colleges Behind Migrant Scam'. *The Times*. https://www.thetimes.co.uk/article/bogus-colleges-behind-migrant-scam-revealed-b3zschblm0s (accessed 2 December 2019).

Fracassini, Camillo. 'Scottish Exams Scam Probe in China'. *Sunday Times*, 30 January 2005. https://www.thetimes.co.uk/article/scottish-exams-scam-probe-in-china-ffrnrmjc3p2 (accessed 2 December 2019).

Francis, Mathew. 2013. 'Harold Wilsons White Heat of Technology Speech 50 Years On'. *The Gaurdian*, 19 September.

GCU (Glasgow Caledonian University). 2012. 'Glasgow Caledonian to Open New York Campus'. Report by corporate author. https://www.gcu.ac.uk/alumni/news/news/article.php?id=64104 (accessed 14 January 2020).

Geoff, Mason, Gareth Williams and Sue Cranmer. 2003. 'Employability Skills Initiatives in Higher Education: What Effect Do They Have on Graduate Labour Market Outcomes'. Institute of Education, University of London, London. http://www.niesr.ac.uk/pubs/DPS/dp280.pdf (accessed 16 April 2019).

Glator, J. D. 2008. 'Investigation into Study Abroad Widens'. *New York Times*, 21 January. https://www.nytimes.com/2008/01/21/us/21cuomo.html (accessed 2 December 2019).

Going Global. 2014. *Impacts of Transnational Education on Host Countries*. Miami: British Council DAAD.

Govt. Press. 2001. 'Eighth Malaysia Plan 2001–2005'. Kuala Lumpur: Government Press.

———. 1976. 'Third Malaysia Plan 1976–80'. Kuala Lumpur: Government Press.

Green, Damian. 2010. Speech given on 6 September at the Royal Commonwealth Society, transcript found at https://www.ein.org.uk/damian-green-real-immigration-question (accessed 30 November 2019).

Green, Madeline. 2017. 'Using Agents to Recruit International Students: A Settled Issue?" NAFSA Trends and Insights, May. https://www.nafsa.org/professional-resources/research-and-trends/using-agents-recruit-international-students-settled-issue (accessed 2 December 2019).

Grove, Jack. 2014. 'QAA Inquiry Says London Campuses Not Ripe for Visa Fraud'. THES, 17 December. https://www.timeshighereducation.com/news/qaa-inquiry-says-london-campuses-not-ripe-for-visa-fraud/2017600.article (accessed 2 December 2019).

Guan, Le Hock. 2014. 'Growth and Change in Financing Malysian Higher Education'. In *Malaysia Socio-Economic Transformation*, ed. Sanchita Basu Das, Singapore: ISEAS-Yusof Ishak Institute, 15.

Havergal, Chris. 2015. 'The Cost of Agents'. *Inside Higher Education*, 12 February. https://www.insidehighered.com/news/2015/02/20/british-universities-are-spending-more-agents-recruit-international-students (accessed 2 December 2019).

HEFC. 2009. 'Diversity in the Student Learning Experience and Time Devoted to Study: A Comparative Analysis of the UK and European Evidence'. HEFC Reports. http://eprints.lse.ac.uk/55682/ (accessed 2 December 2019).

HESA. 'HESA Data Mining Tool'. *SIEM BC*.

———. 2013. 'Hesa TNE Student Data'. HESA.

———. 2018. 'Higher Education Student Data Tool'. BC.

Her Majesty's Inspectorate (HMI). 1989. 'Committee of Enquiry into Teaching Quality'.

———. 1984. 'Engineering in Polytechnics'. London: Her Majesty's Stationery Office (HMSO).

Hillman, Nic. 2019. 'An International Strategy Lacking Ambition', University World News. 30 March.

HM Government Report. 2019. 'International Education Strategy, Global Potential, Global Growth'. https://www.gov.uk/government/publications/international-education-strategy-global-potential-global-growth/international-education-strategy-global-potential-global-growth (accessed 14 January 2020).

Horne, Marc. 2017. 'Scottish University Gets Green Light for US Courses'. *The Times*, 14 June.

House of Commons Home Affairs Committee. 2009. 'Bogus Colleges Report 2009'. Committee report, London: House of Commons.

Hutchinson, Paul. 2016. 'Glasgow Caledonian New York "Campus" Project in Turmoil over US Based Objections'. *The Herald*. 10 October.

———. 2018. 'Glasgow Caledonian University Income from Our New York Campus "Very Disappointing"'. *The Herald*, 18 March.

Hyde, Andrew. 2004. '% of Americans with Passports', *Andrew Hyde Travel Chronicles*. https://andrewhy.de/percent-of-americans-with-passports/ (accessed 6 May 2019).

IHE Report. 2012. 'The State of Things To Come'. British Council, 13 March.

IIE. 2018. 'Open Doors'. iie.org. https://www.iie.org/Research-and-Insights/Open-Doors/Data/International-Students/Enrollment (accessed 10 October 2018).

Institute for Employment Research. 2012. 'Degrees of Advantage? A Longer-Term Investigation of the Careers of UK Graduates'. London: Warwick University.

IPPR. 2012. 'International Students and Net Migration'. London: IPPR.

Jarratt, Alex. 1985. 'Committee of Vice Chancellors and Principals Report of theSteering Comitte for Efficency Studies in Universities'. http://www.educationengland.org.uk/documents/jarratt1985/index.html (accessed 2 December 2019).

Jomo, K. S. 2004. 'The New Economic Policy and Interethnic Relations in Malaysia'. United Nations Research Institute for Social Development. http://www.unrisd.org/unrisd/website/document.nsf/462fc27bd1fce00880256b4a0060d2af/a20e9ad6e5ba919780256b6d0057896b/$FILE/jomo.pdf (accessed 6 January 2019).

Jump, Paul. 2013. 'Evolution of the REF'. *Times Higher Education*, 17 October.

Kearns, R. 2018. 'Why Students in US Colleges Study Abroad'. https://rebeccakearns.wordpress.com/2015/04/13/why-students-in-u-s-colleges-study-abroad/ (accessed 2 December 2019).

Kellner, Peter. 2010. 'Howard, the People's Spy in the Corridors of Power for 50 Years'. The Evening Standard, London. 20 December.

Knight, Jane. 2015. 'Updating the Definition of Internationalisation'. *International Education*, pp. 2–3.

Knight, Jane, and Hans de Wit. 2018. 'What Contribution Has Internationalisation Made to HE?' University World News, 12 October. https://www.universityworldnews.com/post.php?story=20181010093946721 (accessed 14 January 2020).

Labour Party. 2001. '2001 Labour Party General Election Manifesto Ambitions for Britain'. Labour Party. http://labourmanifesto.com/2001/2001-labour-manifesto.shtml (accessed 10 April 2019).

Lea, Susan J., D. Stephenson and J. Troy. 2003. 'Higher Education Students' Attitudes to Student Centred Learning:Beyond Bullimea'. https://www.tandfonline.com/doi/abs/10.1080/03075070309293 (accessed 26 March 2019).

Lee, Hwok-Aun. 2014. 'Malaysian Education, Off Course, Heady Growth, Systematic Woes, Small Fixes'. In *Malaysia's Socio-Economic Transformation*, ed. Sanchita Basu Das, Kuala Lumpur: ISEAS-Yusof Ishak Institute, 337–54. https://muse.jhu.edu/search?action=browse&limit=publisher_id:70 (accessed 2 December 2019).

Lessware, John. 2005. 'Foreign Students Flock to Scotland'. *The Times*, 22 October.

Lewis, J. 1974. 'Finance and the Fate of Polytechnics'. In *Polytechnics: A Report*, ed. Burgess J. Pratt. London: Pitman.

Lewis, V. 2007. ' "Integrated Internationalism" in UK Higher Education: Interpretations, Manifestations'. DBA Thesis.

Malaysia Govt. Press. 1976. 'Third Malaysia Plan'. Third Malaysia Plan: A Plan for National Unity. Kuala Lumpur: National Printing Department.

Malaysian Government. 1957. 'Laws of Malaysia Federal Constitution'. 31 August. http://www.jac.gov.my/images/stories/akta/federalconstitution.pdf (accessed 16 April 2019).

Mathews, David. 2014. 'Glyndwr Planted the Seeds of Its Financial Woes Some Time Ago'. THES, 17 July. https://www.timeshighereducation.com/news/glyndwr-planted-the-seeds-of-its-financial-woe-some-time-ago/2014550.article (accessed 9 June 2019).

May, Theresa. 2011. *Major Changes to Student Visa Sytem*London: Her Majesty's Government. https://www.gov.uk/government/news/major-changes-to-student-visa-system (accessed 19 February 2019).

Mazzarol, T., G. N. Souta. 2002. '"Push-Pull" Factors Influencing International Student Destination Choice'. *International Journal of Educational Management*, vol. 16, no. 2: 82–90.

McConnell, Jack. 2004. 'New Scots Attracting Fresh Talen to Meet The Challenge of Growth'. https://www.webarchive.org.uk/wayback/archive/20180517002043/http://www.gov.scot/Publications/2004/02/18984/33666 (acessed 18 December 2018).

Mehmet, Ozay. 1974. 'Race Riots in Malaysia'. *Queens Quartely*, vol. 81 (January): 4.

Migration Watch UK. 2012. 'Migration Watch Briefing Paper 267'. 21 June. https://www.migrationwatchuk.org/briefing-paper/267 (accessed 16 May 2018).

MOE. 1998. 'Action Plan for Invigorating Higher Education Towards the 21st Century'. http://ie.china-embassy.org/eng/Education/t112959.htm (accessed 12 June 2019).

———. 2003. 'Regulations on Foreign Chinese Cooperation in the Running of Schools'. https://www.sinoptic.ch/textes/eco/2003/20030301_PRC_regulations.running.schools.pdf (accessed 13 June 2019).

———. 2004. 'Implementation Measures for Cooperation on Running Schools'. http://english.jiangxi.gov.cn/study/studyinformation/201504/t20150421_1147400.htm (accessed 13 June 2019).

Mullins, Chris. 2009. *A View From the Foothills*. London: Profile Books.

Norfolk, Andrew. 2009. 'Man Given Job of Closing Down Bogus Colleges Sacked from University'. *The Times*, 29 June.

OECD. 2017. 'OECD Data'. *Education Spending*. https://data.oecd.org/eduresource/education-spending.htm (accessed 2 May 2019).

O'Malley, Brendan. 2018. 'White House Discussed Unilateral Ban on Chinese Students'. University World News, 4 October.

Oxford Economics. 2017. 'The Economic Impact of International Students'. Universities UK. https://www.universitiesuk.ac.uk/policy-and-analysis/reports/Pages/briefing-economic-impact-of-international-students.aspx (accessed 16 April 2019).

Pace, I. 2018. 'The RAE and REF'. 3 April. https://ianpace.wordpress.com/2018/04/03/the-rae-and-ref-resources-and-critiques/ (accessed 16 January2019).

Gumport Patricia J., Maria Iannozzi, Susan Shaman and Robert Zemsky. 1997. 'The United States Country Report: Trends In Higher Education from Massification to Post Massification'. http://course.napla.coplacdigital.org/wp-content/uploads/2016/09/Trends-in-Higher-Education-from-Massification-to-Post-Massification.pdf (accessed 17 January 2019).

Peterkin, Tom. 2004. 'McConnells Big Idea on Migration Ridiculed'. *The Telegraph*, 22 May, p. 12.

Pratt, John. 1997. 'The Polytechnic Experiment 1965–1992'. The Society for Research into Higher Education. London: Taylor and Francis.

QAA. 2014. 'London Campuses of UK Universities: Overview Report of a Thematic Enquiry by the Quality Assurance Agency for Higher Education'. https://dera.ioe. ac.uk/21786/1/London-campuses-of-UK-universities.pdf (accessed 17 Feburary 2019).

Quality Assurance Agency for Higher Education. 2004. 'Code of Practice for the Assurance of Academic Standards in Higher Education. Section 2: Collaborative Provision.

———. 2010. 'Code of Practice for the Assurance of Academic Standards in Higher Education. Section 2: Collaborative Provision. Amplified Version. October. https:// dera.ioe.ac.uk/1197/1/collab2010.pdf (accessed 14 January 2020).

———. 2015. 'Characteristic Statement: Qualifications Involving More Than One Degree Awarding Body'. https://dera.ioe.ac.uk/24584/1/Joint-Degree-Characteristics-15.pdf (accessed 14 January 2020).

Ratcliffe, Mike. 2018. 'Moremeansbetter'. https://moremeansbetter.wordpress.com/ author/mike1ratcliffe/page/2/ (accessed 21 March 2019).

———. 2017. 'The End of the Binary Divide Reflections on 25 Years of the 1992 Act'. WonkHE. https://wonkhe.com/blogs/analysis-25-years-on-the-higher-and-further-education-act-1992/ (accessed 11 December, 2018).

Ratcliffe, Mike, 2018. 'John Major and Academic Drift'. https://moremeansbetter. wordpress.com/tag/history/ (accessed 17 February 2018).

Richmond, Tom. 2018. 'A Degree of Uncertainty'. Think tank, Reform. http://www. tom-richmond.com/wp-content/uploads/2018/06/A%20Degree%20of%20 Uncertainty.pdf (accessed 18 April 2019).

Robbins, Lord. 1963. 'The Robbins Report (1962) Higher Education Report of the Committee Appointed by the Prime Minister under the Chairmanship of Lord Robbins (1961–63)'. London: Her Majesty's Stationery Office.

Robinson, Eric. 1968. *The New Polytechnics*. London: Penguin.

Ledworth, S. and D. Seymour. 2000. 'Home and Away Preparing Students for Multicultural Management'. *Journal of Business Studies*, vol. 3: 34–38.

Sanderson, David. 2017. 'New York Gets Tough Over Scottish University Invader'. *The Times*, 29 May.

Scottish Government. 2006. 'Scotlands Strategy For a Wider Engagement in China'. https://www.research.ed.ac.uk/portal/files/75957048/Scotland_China_strategy. pdf (accessed 12 December 2018).

———. 2017. 'Scottish Government Committees SQA Written Evidence'. March. https://archive.parliament.scot/s3/committees/europe/documents/Writtenevidence-2DecSQAWEB.pdf (accessed 10 October 2018).

Secretary for Education. 2011. 'United States Department of Education: Office of Postsecondary Education'. 11 March. https://ifap.ed.gov/dpcletters/attachments/ GEN1105.pdf (accessed 15 November 2019).

Sevastopulo, Demetri. 2018. 'US Considering Ban on Visas For Chinese Students'. *Financial Times*, 2 October.

Sharma, Yojana. 2012. 'China to Evaluate Foreign University Presence and Prepare Guidelines'. University World News, 22 January.

Shattock, Michael. 2010. *Managing Successful Universities*. Milton Keynes: Open University Press.

————. 2012a. *Making Policy in British Higher Education 1945–2011*. Milton Keynes: Open University Press.

————. 2012b. 'University Governance: An Issue for Our Time'. *Perspecives*, 16: 56–61.

Sherriff, Lucy. 2017. 'So Glasgow Caledonian University Has a Campus in New York. But There Are No Students''. *Huffington Post*, 12 March.

Students and Universities – Innovation, Universities, Science and Skills Committee Contents. 2009. Standards and Quality Committee. https://publications. parliament.uk/pa/cm200809/cmselect/cmdius/170/17008.htm (accessed 12 January 2019).

The Education Reform Act. 1988. The National Archives. http://www.legislation.gov. uk/ukpga/1988/40/contents (accessed 16 September 2018).

THE (Times Higher Education). 1997. 'Manual Staff Underpaid Overstressed and Ignored'. *Times Higher Education*. https://www.timeshighereducation.com/news/manual-staff-underpaid-overstressed-and-ignored/100344.article (accessed 15 November 2018).

The National Archives. 1999. 'Department of Innovation and Skills Archived 9th Feb 2009'. *PMI*. https://webarchive.nationalarchives.gov.uk/+/http://www.dius.gov. uk/international/pmi/index.html (accessed 16 November 2019).

The Telegraph. 2014. 'Tony Benn Dies: His Most Memorable Quotes'. 14 March. https:// www.telegraph.co.uk/news/politics/labour/10697145/Tony-Benn-dies-his-most-memorable-quotes.html (accessed 13 January 2020).

Thomson, Barney. 2019. 'Students' Bank Accounts Frozen Amid Money Laundering Concerns'. *Financial Times*, 28 February.

Transparency International. 2019. 'Corruption Perception Index'. https://www. transparency.org/research/cpi/overview (accessed 21 November 2018).

UCAS. 2015. 'End of Cycle Report'. https://www.ucas.com/corporate/data-and-analysis/ucas-undergraduate-releases/ucas-undergraduate-analysis-reports/ucas-undergraduate-end-cycle-reports (accessed 14 January 2020).

————. 2018. 'UCAS End of Cycle Report 2018'. https://www.ucas.com/data-and-analysis/undergraduate-statistics-and-reports/ucas-undergraduate-end-cycle-reports/2018-end-cycle-report (accessed 20 February 2019).

UKBA. 2010. 'Post Study Work Visa'. London: Her Majesty's Government.

UKCISA. 2004. 'International Students in UK Universies and Colleges: Broadening Our Horizons'. https://warwick.ac.uk/fac/cross_fac/globalpeople/resourcebank/researchpapers/ukcosa_survey_report.pdf (accessed 12 December 2018).

————. 2012. 'PMI Student Experience Achievements 2006–2011'. https://ukcisa. org.uk/Research--Policy/Resource-bank/resources/28/PMI-Student-Experience-Achievements-2006-2011 (accessed 12 January 2019).

UK Parliament Hansard. 2014. https://hansard.parliament.uk/Commons/2014-06-24/debates/14062429000001/StudentVisas (accessed 14 January 2020).

UK Visa Bureau. 2012. 'Teesside University Becomes First to Fall Foul of New UK Visa Rules'. 22 March. https://www.visabureau.com/news/teesside-university-becomes-first-to-fall-foul-of-new-uk-visa-rules (accessed 17 December).

UNESCO. 2018. 'UNESCO Institute for Stastistics'.Outbound Internationally Mobile Students. http://data.uis.unesco.org/Index.aspx?queryid=172 (accessed 16 November 2019).

UNIPAGE. 2019. https://www.unipage.net/en/universities?city_id%5B0%5D= 5128581&per-page=50 (accessed 16 November 2019).

Universities UK. 2011. 'Response to the Student Immigration System – a Consultation'. https://www.universitiesuk.ac.uk/policy-and-analysis/reports/Documents/2011/ response-to-the-student-immigration-system.pdf (accessed 29 November 2019).

———. 2018. 'Paterns and Trends in UK Higher Education 2018'. Universities UK. https://universitiesuk.ac.uk/facts-and-stats/data-and-analysis/Pages/Patterns-and-trends-in-UK-higher-education-2018.aspx (accessed 14 January 2019).

University World News. 2011. 'China to Evaluate Foreign University Presence and Prepare Guidelines that Meet National Needs'. March. https://www.universityworldnews. com/post.php?story=20120118202525930 (accessed 14 January 2020).

Vita, G. De. 2006. 'Inclusive Approaches to Effective Communication and Active Participation in the Intercultural Classroom'. *Active Learning in Higher Education*, vol. 1, no. 2: 12–24.

Welch, A. R. 1997. 'The Peripatetic Professor: The Internationalisation of the Academic Profession'. *Higher Education*, vol. 34: 323–45.

Willets, David. 2013. 'International Education Global Growth and Prosperity', published by HM Government. https://dera.ioe.ac.uk/18071/13/bis-13-1081-international-education-global-growth-and-prosperity_Redacted.pdf (accessed 29 November 2019).

Williams, Geoff, and Sue Crammer. 2006. *Employability Skills Initiatives in Higher Education: What Effect Do They Have on Graduate Labour Market Outcomes Mason*. London: National Institute for Economic and Social Research, 2006.

workpermit.com. 2005. 'England Announces Its Own Fresh Talent Initiative'. 12 December. https://workpermit.com/news/england-launch-its-own-fresh-talent-scheme-20051212 (accessed 29 November 2019).

Wyness, Gill. 2010. 'Policy Changes in Higher Education Funding'. Institute of Education, 1963–2009. https://repec.ucl.ac.uk/REPEc/pdf/qsswp1015.pdf (accessed 21 March 2019).

Yilmaz, Yesim. 2010. *Higher Education Institutions in Thailand and Malaysia – Can They Deliver?* Washington, DC: World Bank.

Zaaba, Zuraidah, Ibiana Florinciliana, Niane Anthony and Haijon Gunggut. 2010. 'English as a Medium of Instruction in the Public Higher Education Institution: A Case Study of Language-in-Education Policy in Malaysia'. https://www.researchgate. net/profile/Zuraidah_Zaaba/publication/228826470_English_as_a_Medium_ of_Instruction_in_the_Public_Higher_Education_Institution_A_Case_Study_of_ Language-in-Education_Policy_in_Malaysia/links/0deec537f0bbb7ec6f000000/ English-as-a-Medium-of-Instruction-in-the-Public-Higher-Education-Institution-A-Case-Study-of-Language-in-Education-Policy-in-Malaysia.pdf?origin=publication_ detail (accessed 19 September 2018).

INDEX

Lightning Source UK Ltd.
Milton Keynes UK
UKHW012033130320
360322UK00001B/24

9 781785 271168